Trousering Your Weasel

Murr Brewster

*For Betsy —
STRIDER of the PLANET! *

Murr Brewster

* and Healer of the Dave.

Contents

Introduction   7

Chapter 1: Ripped From The Headlines

Assault And Badgery   13

It Takes Stones To Wear Curling Pants   15

Flyer, Flyer, Pants On Fire   19

What Creek Is This? And Where's My Paddle?   21

Eager Greeter   25

Personal Horticulture   27

Rest In Pieces   29

It Makes It Easier To Clutch   33

The Woes City   35

Drug Trials   37

Chapter 2: Historical Murr

A Flap Of Skin   43

Bring Your Child To Work Day   47

Torture, And The Rack   51

Born To Mosey   55

When Lizards Fly   57

Road Tripping   61

Curses! Soiled Again   63

Snow Cone Boy   67

This Bud's For You   69

Whey To Go   73

Chapter 3: Science, Nature, Poop.

A Putty Good Idea 81

Requiem For A Biology Degree 85

The Squeeze On Evolutionary Theory 87

Weed vs. Weeds 91

Hot Shit 95

Stop And Smell The Putrescine 99

Iguano 101

To Boldly Go 103

Traveling Light 107

Cool Beans 111

Chapter 4: What In Tarnation

Butt Load 115

The Electronic Leash 117

Look Out! It's A Cycle Path! 121

Toot! Toot! All Aboard The Colonoscopy Bus! 123

Things That Drop Out Of The Sky 127

Just Breathe Normally 131

Staying Up For The Game 133

To Form A More Fabulous Union 137

Where Does The Dime Go? 139

Ticketmonster 143

Chapter 5: Fun With Dave

Blood, Simple 149

Next, A Moose Head 153

The Poot 155

Dispatch From The Belfry 159

Hard Workers Never Pump Their Own   161
A Bunny Tale   165
The Ants Are Back   167
Vampires Among Us   169
The Whiz Kid   173
I Incyst   177

Chapter 6: The Present Murr

A Cure For Cancer   181
A Hell Of A Potter   183
Late-Breaking Mews   187
Under Cover In West Virginia   189
Die Hard, With A Backpack   193
Merriweather   197
The Numbers Racket   201
Pinned Down   205
Music Of The Spheres   209
Round Feet   211

Chapter 7: Fun With Death

A Grave Matter   217
Abbie Normal   221
Bad Day At The Zoo   225
On Being A Foot Shorter   227
Hot In Portland   229
Loved Ones, With A Side Of Lefse   233
The Mortal Coil Shuffle   235
Murr: It's What's For Dinner   239
You Can't Keep A Good Man Down   241
Nearly Beloved   245

Introduction

Not long ago, a man was shot in the state of Montana. Actually, in the arm. He had been traveling the country collecting material for his book on the kindness of strangers. And then, blammo, he was up and shot. Naturally, it made the news.

Within days, it was discovered that he had shot himself in order to get publicity for his book. Police were immediately suspicious when no one came forward to claim credit for popping a cap in the author-boy, in a county where they totally would have expected someone to. Also, he confessed.

None of this surprises me. It's tough to make it as a writer. These days only four people a year are published by the traditional companies, and two of them are Dan Brown. The rest of them have discovered the world of self-publishing, where, for a few hundred bucks, or less if they skimp on grammar and syntax, they can fling out literally dozens of copies of their very own books to a select audience with whom they share genetic material. Each published book is a proud plankton flagellating away in the sea of literature, and the writers struggle to be noticed, let alone paid. "Please like my author page," they beg their friends on Facebook. It's pathetic. I have too much pride for that. Well, it's not pride so much as I have a little pension.

Anyway, I have no intention of pulling such a stunt to promote *Trousering Your Weasel*. Any small mammals you hear about waltzing around in my pants are there for recreational purposes only.

So, let's see. Acknowledgments. I would like to thank my mother. I would *like* to, but she's no longer with us. Obviously, if it were not for my mother, none of these words could have been written. Although quite a few of them wouldn't have been written if she were still alive to read them. I would also like to thank my husband Dave for expert care and feeding of the author, but he gets his own chapter, so there's really no need to keep sucking up. I thank Pat Lichen of Chrysalis Women Writers for threatening to sit on me if I didn't come up with at least 25 illustrations; and my niece Elizabeth Brewster for insisting (with what you might call a "tone") that I had to draw something for *every* piece.

That leaves Big Dave and his wife Vivi to thank. David Gerritsen was one of the first people we netted when we bought a rental house next door and stocked it with useful young people. Big Dave, like many, many before him, listened to me whine about how I thought I was a writer, even though I never wrote anything down. But unlike everyone else, he assigned me an essay. He offered me a stark choice of two options, one of which was "get off the pot," and I chose the other one. After forty years of holding in words, what resulted was a dense, stiff plug of an essay. But once that was out of my system the words just kept spurting right out, and nothing seems to stop them.

And Vivi! Vivian Reidler Gerritsen is as smart as she is beautiful (that is she, posing as my Russian Blonde on page 142). And even better, she could make me laugh in three languages, if I knew the other two. Vivi is the reason you are looking at a book now, rather than a stapled manuscript printed on one side that goes faint green every fifty pages when the ink runs out. I had been staring at the self-publishing site for a good long time when Vivi found me kicking it sullenly, saying "make it go." Vivi made it go, and jammed in my illustrations and sparkled it all up. She's a multi-national treasure and a wonder, and she's got a great rack, besides.

Trousering Your Weasel is a collection of essays from my website Murrmurrs (murrbrewster.blogspot.com), where I have been tacking up humor posts twice a week since 2009. Per my motto, it is my goal to make each piece "snortworthy," but I'm not particular. If I can get any of your bodily fluids on the move, I will have considered my shift on this planet a success. Please like my book.

Murr Brewster

Chapter 1

Ripped From The Headlines

Assault And Badgery
It Takes Stones To Wear Curling Pants
Flyer, Flyer, Pants On Fire
What Creek Is This? And Where's My Paddle?
Eager Greeter
Personal Horticulture
Rest In Pieces
It Makes It Easier To Clutch
The Woes City
Drug Trials

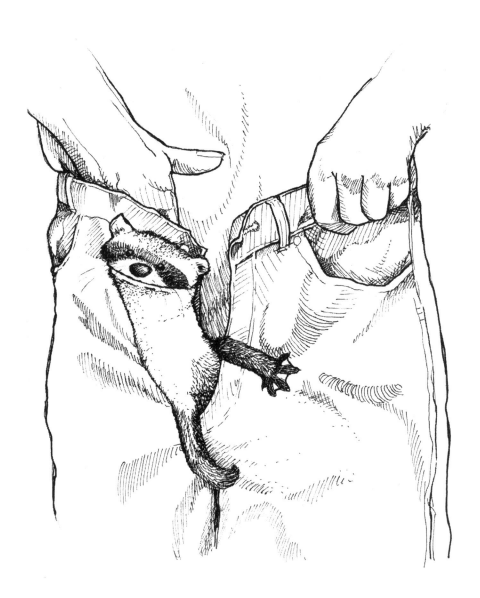

Assault And Badgery

In news from Florida, a homeless man was arrested after he stuffed a ferret in his pants and ran from a pet store.

Although ferret abduction is still relatively rare, store personnel had been on the alert after a Sarasota Petco lost its entire hamster supply inside a pair of cargo pants, although in that case the thief was arrested in short order after police were able to follow a trail of hamster doots all the way to his home. The ferret felon was apprehended in the parking lot of the pet store by an alert teenager, who suffered facial injuries when the thief whipped the ferret out of his pants and brandished it at the young man. The ability to quick-draw a ferret is quite a specialized one and law enforcement officials theorize that the perpetrator had probably practiced the move (called "weaseling out" in ferret-smuggling circles) before. The assault resulted in an additional charge of ferret-wielding on top of the original theft.

In modern times we have become complacent about this sort of threat. The old stoat-totin' days of the wild, wild West are, after all, long gone. Nevertheless there has been a rise in bat-wielding gangs, and a Montana woman recently suffered a severe nibbling at the hands of a miscreant carrying a concealed pika.

Sociologists contacted for this story agree that a predisposition towards pants-ferreting is observed early in life, with ants as the gateway animal, progressing over time to a series of small rodents and ultimately to your larger vertebrates.

It is difficult to say with certainty what the abductor had in mind. The stolen ferret was valued at $129, but authorities do not believe that a fenced hot ferret would fetch enough on the street to justify the considerable risk involved with trousering a weasel. Moreover, it does not seem to be the sort of crime that would go unnoticed. It is this last observation that may hold the key to the matter. A man with a ferret in his trousers may indeed be noticed, but he is rarely approached and questioned. In fact, studies show that test subjects with small mammals in their britches have a distinctly repellent effect on bystanders. The working conjecture in law enforcement is that a homeless man thus equipped would, nine times out of ten, be able to board a bus without paying fare, as well as getting an entire bench seat to himself.

In related news, the Obama administration today denied allegations by the group "Gophers, Guts And Glory" that it plans to confiscate weasels used for personal defense. "Jeez Louise," Mr. Obama was heard to say off-mike, whereupon a spokesman for the President assured correspondents for Fox News that he was not angry, nor taking a tone.

It Takes Stones To Wear Curling Pants

2010. This year the Winter Olympics happened in our time zone. This means we don't get to watch *anything* live. At eight p.m. the television begins to emit a steady stream of stale events, from which we can pick and choose. Figure skating is always a treat: will American favorite Lurleen Neewack be able to land the elusive quadruple-splatchnatz with the triple-putz combination, or will it be revealed, upon reviewing the tape, that she came down .275 degrees past a quarter-turn on her landing skate and thus 2.3 seconds before she actually lifted off, a disqualification? Who cares? The spectator is there to see the efforts of the costumer, fresh off a stint fashioning bridesmaids' outfits for parrots. He is facing stiff competition from the Russian team designer, who, with sequins, feathers, and several yards of baggy flesh-tone material, was able to rock the Australian Aboriginal Shar-Pei theme. From home, it looked like a toss-up.

Outfits are a perfectly reasonable way to decide what to watch when dipping into Winter Olympics coverage. And that is what has drawn so many of us to that fine sport for which Curling Pants were created. We don't even want to know what Curling Pants do. We'd rather speculate. However some understanding of the rules of Curling helps to better appreciate the sport.

Curling was invented in Scotland, shortly after the discovery of heavy drinking. Each curling team consists of four members: the thrower, the skip, and two tidiers. The thrower releases a jelly doughnut made of granite with a handle on it (a "stone"), and it travels across the ice, coming to rest as close to the center of a target at the end of the sheet as possible. In order to influence the speed and trajectory of the stone, two team members aggressively tidy the ice in front of it. Stones may ricochet off other stones, displacing them, and points are awarded according to the number of stones ultimately closest to the target. It is essential for the thrower to release the stone before it passes over the "hog line," a determination that used to be made on the honor system, but in competitive curling a special stone is now used that electronically

detects if the thrower's hand is still on the stone. An electric field at the hog line will detect any infraction and cause the stone to light up like a UFO. This was designed to eliminate the need for an official, to avert controversy, and perchance to reduce hooliganism among the spectators. Sadly, the 2010 Olympic Curling Event was still not hooligan-free, and plans are underway for the 2014 event for a special stone that will cause the thrower to burst into flame upon violation. At the other end of the sheet, the skip's job is to hop up and down and scream at the other members of the team, and occasionally to finish tidying. Each team throws eight stones.

All the rest of the events can be reliably ranked by how closely they resemble curling. Bobsledding, for instance, also features teams of four, and requires a lot of stones. The first man in the bobsled is the "driver," and the second through fourth are the "meat."

Even closer to the ideal of curling is the Women's Giant Slalom, in which racers are sent down the mountain every fifteen seconds or so, allowing later racers to carom off the previously crumpled or deceased entrants, and the team with the most members arriving right-side up at the bottom of the hill wins the gold.

But our heart remains with the curling competitors, especially Canadian home-town hero Cyril "Syrup" Parfait, of Vancouver, B.C., whose parents, having seen his early promise, quit their jobs as neurophysicist and Prime Minister in order to accompany their son to the best Jamaican training facility, where they eked out the money for his coaching by taking jobs licking gym floors. It appeared that M. et Mme. Parfait would not be able to afford to attend the Olympics to cheer their son on, but thanks to the generosity of the good folks at Winnipeg Whack-A-Moose, someone was able to swing by in a Dodge Caravan and pick them up.

Flyer, Flyer, Pants On Fire

It's hard to work up a heap of sympathy for your average suicide bomber, but I felt a twinge for the fellow who failed to detonate his underpants on that flight into Detroit. If I were planning to go out in a blaze of glory, I wouldn't want my underpants to survive me, either. And don't think it couldn't happen. On New Year's Day a few decades ago here in Portland, a fellow opened up the gas line to his house and blew it to smithereens. I was two miles away, and it was still the loudest sound I'd ever heard. There was nothing left of his house but the mortgage, and he took out the neighbors' houses, too, but there he was, dead in his yard, fully intact in his underpants. They probably weren't even riding up.

I don't think men's underpants do ride up. I never see men making an adjustment or anything. Oh, they may fiddle around in there, but it's always the package they're fiddling with, not the wrapping. A female suicide bomber would have been a complete success. If we were supposed to add a liquid to the explosive powder in our underpants, we could do that during a tea party with the Queen and no one would ever know. Every day requires a minimum of several dozen such surreptitious adjustments. We've got it down.

As a letter carrier, I had to slide out of the tall driver's seat onto the pavement all day long, and the entire left side of my underpants disappeared every time. It only took a few steps to arrange my satchel as a shield and perform the extraction, with no one the wiser.

Then I'd start walking my beat, and my recently-thwarted underpants would get bored and irritable. So they would scout out the

19

territory until, within a block, they had located the exact largest circumference on my ass, and then they'd settle in and make a nice indentation to flag the spot, because they did not yet have sequin-and-flashing-lights technology. There they would remain, snug as the Tropic of Capricorn, with all of Brazil pooching out to the north. You can tug them back to the equator and make it look like you're just stretching your back, but you'll be doing it all day long.

Women of a certain age that is not mine wear thong underwear, in part, to avoid this particular constriction. Well, if that ain't like curing insomnia with a whack upside the head, I don't know what is. A deliberate wedgie is still a wedgie. No thank you, Junior. It's hard enough taking my clothes off some days without having to excavate.

To really put the cherry on top of the whole underwear experience, though, you must add tights. Tights are sold in a variety of sizes, none of them mine. I am parked on the cusp, and my choices are to tuck the tights under my bra and watch them puddle up at the ankles, or get the ones that come out of the dryer eighteen inches long and fit like a sausage casing.

There is, however, no avoiding "control-top" hose, even if you were not planning to ask anything of your underwear you do not ask of yourself. Control-top hose is made of Spandex, a synthetic fiber developed by bored and irritable Nazis. The function of the control-top is to round up fat wherever it is hiding and shoot it out the top. The effect is that of a billowing flesh fountain on a nylon pedestal, and gosh—ain't that the look we were going for, ladies? Comfy, too. It takes five minutes to argue them all the way up to the waist, but sadly, fifteen minutes later, the tights have retreated to new ground quite a bit south of ideal. Enforcing a waddling gait, the crotch is now hanging six inches below your own, and no, you have nothing to fill that space up with. Not unless you have explosive powder.

What Creek Is This? And Where's My Paddle?

It was April, 2010. A distant rumbling was followed several minutes later by a sustained ralphing noise. As we all know by now, of course, that sound was issuing from the Bartelheimer Brothers Dairy in Snohomish, Washington, where a lagoon containing 21,000,000 gallons of liquefied cow manure ruptured and emptied its contents into the fields and then into the French Slough, a tributary of the Snohomish River. (Efforts are already underway to change the name of the French Slough to reflect current popular usage, according to Darryl Dimrod, the widely-grinning proprietor of Snohomish Paddles-R-Us.)

This is a poop breach of almost unimaginable proportions, although, speaking personally, it does bring to mind a certain difficult afternoon in late November, 1975, and doesn't it suck to be a bicycle commuter sometimes?

As yet there is no explanation for the massive failure of the dike. "It's a known hazard," admitted a local dairyman, intimating that any effort to contain huge quantities of shit is bound to lead to a blowout sooner or later, which has certainly been my experience. But this begs the question why anyone would deliberately maintain a lagoon of 21,000,000 gallons of liquefied cow poop in the first place.

It would be one thing if the lagoon contained 21,000,000 gallons of bird poop—in fact, that would be really something—but whereas cow poop starts out liquid, it tends to jell up right away, like the squirtable mashed potato machine at Denny's. The cow flop then dries up and can be used for cow-pie-throwing contests, home insulation, and notably, fuel. In many areas past and present, cow pies were a primary source of fuel for cooking, which probably took a little of the sting out of your occasional potato famine.

Many animals, such as the llama, the guinea pig, and various birds, are fastidious about their pooping, making an effort to eliminate outside their immediate environments—nests, cages, trails, etc. Cows have never been observed to back up to a lagoon to make deposits, rather, letting the chips fall where they may, and yet they are

just fastidious enough to avoid pasture that they or their friends have pooped in. Evolutionarily speaking, this has led them to be nomadic in nature. In confined areas such as a dairy farm, it is advisable to remove the chips, and bingo, there's your poo-poo pond.

This means that a number of good American jobs are to be had in Dairy Poop Lagoon Maintenance. Several workers must be employed to tip those pasture pastries up on end and roll them up to the lagoon, where, presumably, several more workers are on hand to add water and stir. A third contingent is responsible for coming up with a side dish.

Due to queasiness, I prefer to visualize the first group of employees dressed in short pants and funny hats and rolling the cow pies down the lane with a stick. They would be cheerful and carefree like the sepia-toned children of yore, who rolled hoops in the days before electronic ("real") fun was invented.

Any one of these fine American workers could have been in a position to put his finger in the dike at Bartelheimer Brothers Dairy at the first sign of trouble. He would run the risk of becoming sepia-toned, but it seems to me he would also be in an excellent position to negotiate himself a pretty healthy pay raise.

Eager Greeter

Tell me this hasn't happened to you before. You're standing up to your chest in swamp water next to your niece Elizabeth, who is gazing meditatively into the murk looking for blobs of frog eggs, and just before the sustained shrieking starts, a giant rodent swims right in front of her. It's a nutria, in all likelihood, according to your niece's exceptionally noisy and high-pitched description of a beaver-headed rat the size of a cocker spaniel, although identification is not certain without a sighting of the bright orange incisors. Really, any time you see something you aren't expecting, it can give you a bit of a start.

That's what happened to one unfortunate and excitable woman when she encountered a nutria padding down the aisles of her local Wal-Mart. For some reason, she wasn't expecting such a thing. Low prices, always; giant orange-toothed rat-tailed beaver-headed rodent in the soda pop aisle, less often. I'm not all that surprised, myself. You can probably get a nutria to work for next to nothing. But our victim was so startled she felt a lawsuit coming on. She was *so* overcome, in fact, that she ran over her own person with her own shopping cart, breaking several of her own bones. She did have a decent case that the Wal-Mart management was aware they were harboring a nutria, inasmuch as all the employees referred to him as "Norman," as in the phrase "oh, that's just Norman." Norman didn't upset *them*, but then again they were expecting to run into him. It's all about the expectation.

Here in Portland, we have a beautiful Japanese bell set up near the Convention Center in its own little pavilion. It's a big handsome bell, and it would be even more attractive if it were not eclipsed by a pair of large signs warning passers-by that it could ring without warning. Well! That's helpful! One might just as well put up signs all over town, saying "Any Second Now, Something Or Other Could Scare You Half To Death." You don't know *which* second, so unless you wanted to commit to a more-or-less perpetual state of anxiety, there's not much you can do. Really, all the sign next to the beautiful bell is saying is "Good Luck Trying To Sue Us Now."

A startled woman in Wal-Mart could run over her own feet, pull down a display of frying pans on her own head, and stab herself repeatedly with a fork in agitation, and she would have had no legal recourse if only the store had posted a "Big Honking Rodent On Aisle Five" sign.

Personal Horticulture

Recently a man was admitted to the hospital in pulmonary distress, and x-rays revealed he had a small pea plant growing in his lung. These things can happen. A friend of mine, Joanie, once checked into the doctor's with respiratory difficulties, got a battery of x-rays and what-have-you, and was just a week away from starting chemo when she sneezed out a fava bean and that was it for her cancer.

So what makes this gentleman's experience so unusual is not that he inhaled a pea but that he was able to grow a pea plant in his lung. Just the right conditions had to prevail. He might never have gotten a start if he hadn't been in the habit of huffing potting soil, and once he snorted the Osmocote it was a done deal.

My friend Tamara is brilliant and beautiful, but the best thing about her is she snorts when she laughs and she laughs all the time. Still, I was astonished when she mentioned she had gone to the emergency room because she had aspirated a piece of linguini. I was astonished because I thought she had already been to the ER several years back for the very same thing. "No, no," she assured me, "that was vermicelli." The girl's just one good pun and some pesto away from growing a lasagna in her lungs, and that's yet another thing I love about her.

I had a good idea I had a hop vine growing out of my liver once, and with good reason, but it turned out to be a pulled muscle. However, if the history of the earth teaches us anything, it's that life will prevail anywhere it gets a foothold. This is why it's so dangerous to eat raw eggs. Medical lights try to scare you away from the prospect by raising the specter of salmonella poisoning, but the real danger is an inadvertent hatch. It's uncomfortable, it's unsightly, and the intestinal crowing can lead to insomnia and loss of companionship.

This is the real reason constipation is so hazardous to your health. If you have an intestine packed with fertile soil that isn't going anywhere, it is essential to get it moving again lest something take root. High-fiber cereal should be ingested immediately, and then the race is on to see whether the obstruction can be moved before you sprout a field of oats. Massage can help. It's touch and go all the way.

An awful lot can go wrong—and you might want to make a note of this—when you put things in the wrong holes. We each have many holes, each with its own dedicated function, although there is some overlap (whistling, for instance). I've done such a careful job minding what goes in my holes, if you don't count the 1970s, that I've even managed to avoid swimming for decades. You would too, if every time you came up for air, you were still underwater. Last thing I need is a bunch of lungfish.

Rest In Pieces

A fin whale beached itself near Florence, Oregon the other day. That hardly ever works out for the whale, and it didn't this time. There's always a lot of speculation over the health, mental and physical, of a stranded whale; what could cause it to heave up on shore? Was it itchy, or morose? Fin whales, being equipped with baleen, eat nothing but small fry and crustaceans, but I've been around long enough to know that sometimes it's the appetizers that will do you in. You get into enough krill, and you just want to go lie down for a while. I'm that way with bean dip.

There was the customary quandary of how you get rid of such a massive dead thing. People are always drawn to these scenes, although I would venture that none of those attracted have ever picked meat out of a mess of crab and discarded the shells into the kitchen wastebasket on a hot July day, thinking it will be okay just overnight. There was talk of towing the whale out to sea, burying it in place, or just leaving it. What there was *no* talk of was the solution that a very bright person came up with in 1970 when the same thing happened in the same area.

That very bright person, a demolitions expert from the highway department—let's call him Sparky—reasoned that if a beached whale was set with enough charges to blast it into meatballs, the gulls would carry it away before it hit the ground. If you've ever gutted a fish while on the ocean and tossed the bits you didn't want into the air, you have found that this is exactly what happens. So it was a very elegant solution from nearly every angle except reality. You can be an expert in a lot of things, but no one is an expert in

everything. In this case, the engineer in question was sadly under-informed about the bodily integrity of the whale. What you think should happen is not necessarily what happens.

Sparky spiked the whale with explosives. The gulls were in attendance in force. So, unfortunately for Sparky, were the news media. The whale was duly detonated, and instead of shrapnel and shards of vaporized whale raining down upon the land, pieces of blubber the size of Volkswagens went airborne and came down upon the citizens and infrastructure of Florence. One chunk came down and cratered a car. Nobody, today, is willing to say it was a fluke.

The entire event was so implausible that, for a time, it entered into the realm of urban mythology, until it was clawed back into its rightful slot in history by those who had been, after all, witnesses. Sort of like the Holocaust.

So our current whale was dug into the sands with minor ceremony. It's a shame. I fear that people will be less inclined to come up with creative solutions to our problems when faced with the possibility of catastrophic humiliation. And we'll just have to come up with some other way of dealing with Rush Limbaugh.

It Makes It Easier To Clutch

The other day, the police pulled over a pantsless man on the freeway. He was doing 69 in a 50-mph zone. However, it was the speeding that got the cops' attention.

When asked, the fellow explained that he had lost his pants. The cops searched the car but didn't find any pants. Well, duh. When I lose my pants, I never look in the car. At least, not since the seventies. Nor do I drive off to look for them. Most of the time, I stay right at home until the condition clears up. If truth be told, most of the time my pants are more abandoned than lost, although it might feel the same to the pants.

However, there are probably many reasons a man might drive around without his pants on, and one of them is surely the reason the man gave. Your whole life shouldn't have to come to a crashing halt just because you lose your pants. Nobody'd get anything done in a world like that. There are still things to do, places to go, people to flash. But it's still a good idea to avoid committing a serious crime under the circumstances, unless you enjoy the attention. Oh, sure, there is a crime for which pantslessness is practically a uniform, but that's an exception.

You hardly ever hear about a bank robber, for instance, who isn't wearing any pants. Whereas it's true that the very act of robbing a bank requires a certain kind of personal equipment, you don't want that equipment to be readily identifiable in a line-up. You're too likely to be fingered.

The Woes City

Portland, Oregon: the month of May has recently adjourned after setting a record of one hundred and forty-five consecutive days of rain, smashing the previous single-month record of eighty-nine days in 1876 ("Dead Man's April"). Portlanders woke up last week to the news that a woman who had jumped from a tall building fell directly on another woman walking underneath on the sidewalk, killing both instantly. Slouching in coffee shops, languidly stroking the ridged scars on their wrists, they pondered, in that crescent of time between the last coffee and the first beer, which of the two women was the most fortunate.

Although suicide pacts among the young have largely been thwarted by lethargy, pedestrians have been observed to linger on bridges. In the animal world, cats are irritable, slugs exhibit zip, and the baby bird population has proven susceptible to drowning, with natural selection now favoring the picky eater.

In those few areas experiencing sunbreaks, rods and cones have snapped audibly; temporary blindness is reported to have led to a spike in fatal car wrecks, some of which have been ruled accidental. Elsewhere, sporadic sunbreaks have been blamed for the socially corrosive introduction of hope.

Sociologists are also studying the possible detriment to the spirit arising from Portlanders' self-satisfaction as environmental advocates, noting that the reputation is largely unearned. Anyone willing to wait a couple years can boast a green roof, they point out. As always, natives spurn the personal use of umbrellas, which merely add to the number of items that require drying out. These are observed only in the days leading up to the Rose Festival to protect hybrid tea roses in competition. Portland is, in fact, known as the Rose City, an umbrella term (as it were) encompassing many individual Black Spot Fungus neighborhoods, and this holds the key to understanding springtime weather patterns in the area.

Traditionally, the Rose Festival concludes with a week of parades in June, beginning with the Starlight Parade, an evening event named after a mythical sky phenomenon. This parade always features a clown troupe called the Rainmakers, who carry inside-out umbrellas and spray spectators with water pistols, an activity that was finally abandoned when nobody noticed. The Grand Floral Parade is held one week later, featuring thousands of plastic-covered spectators lining the streets to witness the annual drenching of delicate petals and princess curls. It's a festive scene, and marks the coming of the sunny season, which begins the next day. Meteorologists explain that our prevailing weather pattern arises when a deep plume of moisture embedded in a powerful jet stream stretching from Japan to the Oregon coast collides with the Rose Festival Grand Floral Parade.

The hail, on the other hand, is thought to be caused by the planting of peonies.

Drug Trials

Says here in the newspaper they've discovered that a drug for stroke victims seems to be helpful for increasing rat brain power. I always thought rats were plenty smart to begin with. It could be I just assumed that they were smart, because they are so unattractive, and on both ends. A lot of times the homeliest kids in class turned out to be the brains, and even the kids who beat them up were careful not to mash them on the head. Rats are homely, so it stands to reason they're writing code in their nests.

They injected middle-aged rats with this stroke drug and were amazed at how smart they became. Rats without the stroke drug became senile at a more rapid pace. I don't know what constitutes a senile rat. I would consider it a mark of senility if the rats repeatedly went into one corner of their cages and then turned around and went back where they started, in an effort to remember what they went into the other corner for to begin with. Then they'd go back to the other corner and forget what they'd remembered and start nosing around in some new scratch. So that's: forth, back, forth, back, nose around. I've had more opportunity than most to observe lab rats and that's pretty much what they do. My colleagues in the laboratory did not mark this as a sign of rat senility, but they were unanimous in their opinion that rats are way smarter than mice. I haven't ruled out the possibility that this is academic mythmaking based on bias against mice, who are kind of cute; cuter, in fact, than my colleagues ever were in grade school, back when they were getting beat up.

I wasn't able to glean from the article why it is we need smarter rats, but in an article on the same page, I learned that another par-

ticularly valuable pharmaceutical is being manufactured from the milk of genetically altered goats. A small subset of humans owes their lives to this drug, but there's a bit of an uproar about the goats. They look okay, but no one really knows what will happen if they were to get out of their pen and mix with the general unaltered goat population. So there's been a call to cease production of the drug. I'm sympathetic to this idea, although it would be a right bummer to have to tell people who want to know how you're doing that you'll be fine just as long as the goat fencing holds. On the other hand, it's not much more tenuous a hold on life than we all have.

You wonder about some of these drug trials. In the same newspaper, it is reported that a whaling ship and an anti-whaling ship got in a stand-off down in Antartica, and the whalers pelted the greenies with chunks of blubber. The whaling ship was only collecting its legal limit of 985 whales for scientific purposes, basically minding its own business. Their scientific inquiry appears to be limited to selling whale at the highest price possible to Japanese consumers, so I guess it's a study in economics, which is considered sort of a science. And if they sell all their whale, they'll have to do it again the next year, and the next, because the study results are more reliable over time. Anyway, my point is the whaler-scientists chunked blubber at the interlopers because that's what they had to chunk with. I suspect sometimes the pharmaceutical scientists just use what they've got, too. They already had a stroke drug, all made up; so they lobbed it at the rats to see what would happen. They happened to smarten up the rats, but think what a bonanza it would have been if the rats had grown thicker, more lustrous fur.

Chapter 2

Historical Murr

~

A Flap Of Skin
Bring Your Child To Work Day
Torture, And The Rack
Born To Mosey
When Lizards Fly
Road Tripping
Curses! Soiled Again
Snow Cone Boy
This Bud's For You
Whey To Go

A Flap Of Skin

My daddy knew everything. You could ask him why the sky was blue or why the leaves turned colors or what the name of that mushroom was and he would tell you, right down to the wavelengths and the refraction and the chromatophores and so on. So when I asked how you could tell a boy baby from a girl baby, and the whole room tensed up, I didn't really notice. I was pretty sure he had the answer. Just that right then wasn't a good time.

It was easy enough to tell boys from girls at my age because of the clothes and haircuts, but little babies all looked alike. I waited a day or two and then, since I still wanted to know, I asked again. Mom cut Daddy a glance and discovered something urgent to do in another room, and Daddy pulled the drawing paper out of the secretary and got a pencil. He started to draw and explain, but with none of his usual vitality. The salient feature in his illustration—in profile, as I recall—was what he called "a little flap of skin." I looked at the drawing and suddenly remembered how you could tell a boy from a girl, and also that I probably shouldn't have brought it up.

In my defense, at that point I didn't have a lot to go on. My only brother was seventeen years older than me and out of the house. Dad was the sort who buttoned the top button on his pajamas. I didn't have a lot to go on, but I did have Danny Hall.

Danny Hall was the inordinately proud owner of the first little flap of skin I ever saw. He had made a point of showing it to me not that much earlier. It was a curiosity, for sure, but I had no idea what it was for, and hadn't made a connection with that whole boy/girl thing. As far as I knew, it was just something that Danny Hall had. He was always coming up with stuff. I do remember he was interested in what was in my pants, but that struck me as odd. I didn't have anything in my pants, not that you could point to, or with.

Besides, as gullible as I tended to be, I was getting to where I didn't trust Danny Hall that much. Even if you couldn't figure out what he was up to, you could be pretty sure it was no good. That same summer he had found a plain white rock and he held it out to me and told me to lick it. Even though I hadn't figured out it was a petrified dog turd at that point, I didn't lick it. Because why would I lick a stone? Especially one of Danny's stones.

The Halls lived on the end of the block, and they had a giant mimosa tree that was gorgeously climbable even to abbreviated sorts like myself. We used to play over there a lot; we had to make up our own games, because plastic and electricity hadn't been invented yet. It was a wholesome time. So mostly, we played World War Three. This involved a lot of hiding behind bushes and spying and such. That's what we were playing when Danny lobbed a brick way up into the air and it came down on my head, and don't think I can't still show you exactly where it landed. I wasn't much of a crybaby but I screamed bloody murder. The closest grown-up, unfortunately, was weird Mr. Balderson, who snatched me into his kitchen, clipped out a bunch of my hair and began boiling washcloths and applying them to my head. By the time my mom intervened, I was still bleeding, newly scalded and hadn't stopped bawling. Danny Hall was apprehended and brought in to defend himself, squirming in his closely-gripped shirt. He had a defense, all right. "I *yelled* BOMBS OVER TOKYO!" he protested, all innocence.

So back to Danny's penis. Danny's penis reminded me of nothing so much as one of those little valves you blow up a vinyl inner tube with. I didn't say that out loud, which, in retrospect, was probably a good idea, because Danny was the sort who might have sensed an opportunity. Anyway, it was his flap of skin that popped into my head when Daddy drew his somber little picture. I got it right away. I wished I'd asked him about the phases of the moon instead.

I didn't keep track of Danny. I did hear, later, he had become a hoodlum. Much later, I heard he had become a lawyer.

Bring Your Child To Work Day

It must have been a festive atmosphere at the jail on Bring Your Child To Work Day. There was probably a limit to what could be done to entertain or educate the children, but somebody got the idea to gather them together in a circle, have them hold hands, and—just for yuks, mind you, and a little physics lesson—zap them with a stun gun. I can see how the idea could come to a person. I guess it was quite the event, though. Somebody's mommy got all upset, and felt a lawsuit coming on.

Back when I was coming up, we didn't have Bring Your Child To Work Day. That started in the seventies as a thing just for daughters, but in the fifties our mommies were all at home. Daddies were at work, but with all our needs met at home, we didn't really care, or know, what they did. I still don't know exactly what mine did.

But I do know we could have been lined up and Tasered and no one would have thought to make a federal case out of it. A fair portion of the kids, all of them male, would have thought it was cool, and gone home to see about peeing on a battery. An even bigger portion would have reasoned that, whatever it was, they had it coming. Most of us wouldn't have thought of questioning the acts of a grown-up, accepting even derangement as within the norm of adult behavior. And a few, like me, would have figured: hey. At least it's not as bad as Recess.

I liked the idea of going out and playing in the sun for a half-hour as much as the next kid, but in practice Recess was sort of an ordeal. I was always the smallest and youngest kid in class. It was a snap to knock me over. When I was really little, my favorite group

47

game was Duck, Duck, Goose. Mostly that was because it involved getting pats on the head, but there was also the giddy anticipation building up as to who would be the Goose, although it was usually me. No child in history ever tapped me for Goose and got caught. For one thing, the smack on the head always bowled me over. By the time I got my feet under me and scrambled up, my quarry had already run around the circle and taken my place. But it was still kind of fun.

Then when we got older, we played a lot of games with balls, big turgid balls in public-school red, and that represented a whole new technology with which I could be knocked over remotely. Mind you, I was not only little, but inept. I had already knocked myself down playing tetherball, twice. I was alone both times.

The standard game was kickball. It was played much like base-ball, only—and here's the fun part—you could get a runner out by throwing the ball at her. In the head, hard, if you wanted to; the teachers were all inside smoking. The pitcher would roll the ball towards the kicker, who could request any of the four combinations of slow, fast, smooth, and bouncy. I always called for Slow and Smooth. Otherwise I could get knocked into the backstop. As it was, I had to kick the ball with the side of my foot to keep from crushing my toes. So the ball invariably scooted languidly off my foot in the direction of third base, and was readily scooped up by the pitcher, who had all the time in the world to knock me clean off my slow trajectory towards first.

Other times, the game was just stripped down to its essential and sinister elements: dodge-ball. Here, all the boys whose mothers shopped for them in the Husky department lined up with evil enthusiasm and hurled the missile at each other at close range. As a small and dentable person, I cowered in the back like a sentient tenpin. Theoretically, you were supposed to try to catch the ball, but I could just as easily have snagged a meteor with a guppy net. It made a body look forward to going back inside to study long division.

I'm a grown-up now, and although I am still easily tipped, I no longer worry much about people knocking me down. The Husky boys have grown up too. They're selling cars and hanging sheet-rock and writing briefs. A couple of the ones who were shaving in third grade are probably still out there pounding on people; maybe defending the sanctity of their third, fourth and fifth marriages. But they're leaving me alone.

Torture, And The Rack

As if Saudi women didn't have it bad enough, it turns out that they're not allowed to work in underwear stores, which puts them in a bind. They are mortified by the prospect of discussing underwear with male clerks, so as a consequence many women in Saudi Arabia are wearing the wrong size bras. In this respect, of course, according to Oprah, they are no different from American women.

There are degrees of mortification. Every single bra-shopping trip in my life triggered an aftershock from the initial excruciating episode when I was twelve or so. My family was modest to a fault. I was humiliated by the prospect of bringing up my need for a bra to a woman who, I have no doubt, conceived me immaculately while fully clothed. Eventually, and a bit late in the game, the mortification of not having a bra trumped the other mortification. But neither could hold a candle to the mortification of the actual purchase. As always, both parents were in attendance, my father reluctantly. He was a wonderful man with no ease *whatsoever* in social situations, and unfortunately the bra department maven was someone we knew from church. Daddy hung back uncomfortably, eventually distracting himself by pawing through a basket of silk undies at the counter. "Now, you leave those alone, George!" the bra lady sang out merrily for the benefit of the hard-of-hearing, and Daddy retreated instantly, shamed and miserable. Meanwhile, I was cringing in the dressing room with a bevy of brassieres, blushing all over—it was easy to tell—when the bra lady whipped the curtain open to find out how "we" were doing. She invited herself in and proceeded to give me, and much of the greater metropolitan area, instructions. "Now just bend over, dear, and pour yourself in," she bellowed happily. She loved her job. I tried to pour myself through the floor vent and into another dimension.

From that day on, I did all my bra shopping alone, with mixed results. Nothing I bought was ever all that comfortable, and by the time Oprah came out with the news that most of us were wearing the wrong size bra and could benefit from a professional fitting, I could concede that it was a possibility, albeit one I would never look into. Until one day I was in Nordstrom's, with their frighteningly helpful personnel. I insisted to the clerk that I didn't need any help, but made the mistake of admitting I was looking for something that didn't exist: a comfortable bra. Well! Would I like to be fitted? I would not, but the clerk was already squinting knowledgeably at my chest and pulling bras off the displays, and I let her follow me into the dressing room.

Here's how a fitting works: The fitter puts a tape measure under the breasts, pulls it tight enough to hinder respiration, and takes note of the circumference. That's just for drill. It's the measurement around the forearm that we're going to end up using. The cup size is considerably different from what one is used to, as well. The elastic is robust enough to have drawn in flesh from the sides and back and points south, so we are contending with a lot more volume than before, and a cup size that would be cozy on a missile-head is recommended. A series of bras is produced and installed with the use of a foot planted firmly in the back; the result looks like an exploding tourniquet. Clearly the bra, and its contents, are not going anywhere for a while. So, yes. Like most American women, I have apparently been wearing the wrong size bra, if by "wrong size" you mean a 38-C when it should have been a 22-OMG.

"Now. Don't you look better?" the clerk beams, and begins to take advantage of my inability to inhale by ringing me up. I go home wearing my new correct bra, suspecting that if I ever get it unhooked, it will shoot clear across the room and clip the cat. But we will never know. With even a spot of perspiration, there's no removing the thing. Even if you're highly, highly, highly motivated.

Mostly I prefer to set the girls free in their original packaging nowadays, but it's getting to where that doesn't fit so well, either.

Born To Mosey

They've got this genetic test they can do now so you can find out if your child is likely to excel in athletics. This test is particularly useful if your own observational skills are meager. They look for some kind of gene marker for speed and springiness. You can swab the inside of your child's cheek and send in the DNA to the testing lab and for $160 they'll let you know if he's got potential for zip and is just being lazy, or if you should plan to spend the next eighteen years rolling him over on the sofa to prevent sores.

I suppose this kind of information helps parents with their day-to-day child micromanagement. With one tissue-culture they can find out if they should push the soccer drills and save up for a genuine Rumanian coach, or just buy the kid a clarinet and hope for something better next time.

My parents would have had it easy collecting my DNA, because I move slow and drool. But it would have been a giant waste of time. Testing me for athletic prowess would be like thumping a bowling ball for ripeness. I've never had any skills. If I were ever to excel in an Olympics, it would have to be a special one just for me, featuring trudge-scotch, stationary jumprope, tether-feather, and Red Light Red Light. One thing that was probably a plus for my mother was that she only needed to check on my whereabouts every half hour or so, because I couldn't have gotten far.

It was awful in grade school. Every day at recess the two kids who usually got to be captains chose their teams, and it always got down to me and the kid with flippers. I didn't feel bad for myself.

I had no part of my self-worth tied up in sports ability, but I felt sorry for the captains. I wouldn't have picked me either. They'd stand there, shifting their weight from foot to foot, all anguished, and finally one would say "oh, I guess I'll take *him*," and the flippered kid would hitch on over, and the remaining captain would close his eyes in resignation.

I was exciting to watch in softball games, although it put the coach on edge. If I was on second base, there was always the possibility the batter would lap me before I made it home, and technically you're not supposed to score the fourth run before the third. I read an article about the genetic differences between good athletes and us more torpid specimens, and took some comfort in it. It turns out that muscles are made up of slow-fire and quick-fire fibers, and the ratio of these is more or less set at birth. "So the sprinters naturally have a greater proportion of quick-fire muscle strands," I read to Dave. He looked at me and said, eschewing the minced word, "you don't have *any* of those."

He has plenty. He runs bases like he's an electron, and it's a good thing, too, because the boy has a mouth on him. I, on the other hand, have had to develop my powers of ingratiation. Pokiness helps hone a sense of humor. You might be just as mean and opinionated as the next guy, but if you can manage to be adorable about it, people let you get away with stuff.

So I can't see my parents shelling out for a genetic test for athletic ability. I can see them watching me execute a crumpled cartwheel or throwing a ball at my own feet and thinking: maybe she can draw.

When Lizards Fly

Thirty years ago, I lived with a two-foot-long iguana and Dave. Both of them had the run of the house. Both were creatures with simple, straightforward needs, which I find soothing. Sparky, the iguana, was a heat-seeker. It's a reptile thing. They get most of their energy from external sources, and if you are warm, they will be happy to crawl on you and soak up some heat. Lizard owners interpret this as affection, and maybe they're right. If someone comes to you for his basic needs, you might just as well call it love as anything else.

So most of the time, when we looked around for Sparky, she was in the same places: the coils on the back of the refrigerator, the radiator, or spread across the top of a floor lamp with her tummy over the light bulb. One day, we couldn't find her in any of her usual haunts. But we knew she'd turn up, so we went to bed. And there she was, on top of a curtain valance. No doubt she had climbed up there to bask in the sun, and as dusk fell, she got colder and colder, eventually becoming too chilly to motivate back down.

Dave, who is a warm mammal and a nice guy, plucked Sparky, now rigid, from the valance, and gallantly stuffed her under his T-shirt. She didn't move much at first, but as his belly heat began to take effect, she started to come alive. Just about the time he was beginning to look like the victim in the movie Alien, he reached beneath his shirt to extract the iguana and snap her back onto the refrigerator coils. But Sparky had lots of energy by then, and reacted by scooting up his chest and into his armpit.

I'd never known the man to be ticklish before, but there he was, a long green tail hanging out of the front of his shirt, and a fringed green head poking out of his sleeve, and he was hopping up and down and squeaking like an old bedspring. I had the same reaction to this scene as anyone would. Wouldn't this be a great time for the Jehovah's Witnesses to drop by?

You can't always get what you want, but sometimes you can come close. At a time in my life when I thought it was impolite to tell a salesperson that I wasn't interested, I opened the door for an alarmingly fragrant Avon lady and agreed to let her show me her potions. She sat on my sofa with her sample box, a bright red smile on her orange face, and I knew she didn't have a thing I wanted.

Anyone could tell I was not a woman who spent money on cosmetics. To an Avon lady, however, I looked like someone who really, really needed to spend money on cosmetics. She examined my face, which was innocent of makeup, and offered me a selection of products with which I could achieve the natural look.

As the minutes wore on, I knew I would have to find something to buy so she would not have wasted her time. Soon an array of skin cream samples dotted the sofa between us. I poked around at them looking for something that didn't smell too much. And that is the moment Sparky, who had, unbeknownst to me, been biding her time on the top of the curtain, plummeted gracefully through the air and landed *plop* on the sofa between us. The Avon lady shot straight up six inches and squeaked like an old bedspring; she came back down and bounced the lizard back up in the air, and so on and so forth; dozens of tiny jars of skin cream sprayed into the air and rolled onto the carpet. She left soon after, tucking my order for a lifetime supply of face goo into her briefcase.

She never came back with my order. My check cleared. It was totally worth it.

Road Tripping

Back when I was a tadpole, our mothers used to broom us out the back door and tell us to roll around in the dirt, eat grubs and play kickball in traffic. We lived by our wits, such as they were. Ultimately, this led my entire generation to engage in a little thing called a "road trip," wherein groups of large children who had obtained sexual maturity, if nothing else, piled into cars and took off for the hills. Maps were free from the gas station, but the cars were guaranteed to fail, telephones were scarce, there were no machines that spit out money, and, for that matter, there was no such thing as a credit card. Survival was all up to you and whatever common sense and resourcefulness you had accumulated through the years of parental neglect. Drugs and alcohol upped the ante. Natural selection worked as it was intended to, and those of us who remain topside are more or less able to think for ourselves.

Things are different now. Children are carefully supervised, padded against danger and sent out with wicking underwear and weatherproof outfits and enough electronics to replace every part of their brains. A child plunked down in the wilderness now would spin in place for a few hours, and then make an art project out of acorns and mud and wait for praise from the rescuers. This method of child-rearing produces grownups like the ones here in Oregon who, last month, headed down unmaintained roads in the grip of winter until they got stuck, far from civilization, because that's what the little voice on their GPS system told them to do. The modern version of the old saw is no longer rhetorical. "If Garmin told you to go jump off a cliff, would you jump off a cliff?" *Why, yes! Yes we would!*

One stranded couple knew exactly how to get over the mountain to their destination, but they faltered when the GPS lady insisted they take a short cut. The GPS lady was so sure of herself that, when they passed by the shortcut because they couldn't see it, since it was *all covered in snow*, she admonished them to make a U-turn. Which they did, and proceeded to plow their way into a snowy oblivion several miles in. Their cell phones didn't work, either. This poor family was so baffled by the failure of their electronic neuron supply that they did the only thing they could think of. They made a nice video of their surroundings and waited to die.

Technology may be a snap if you're born to it, but it can be very frustrating to those who had been raised to rely on their own brains. We will never forget the scene of Dave's mom crouching in front of the oven one Thanksgiving. That fine woman had, by then, roasted about fifty Thanksgiving turkeys in her life with complete success, but there she was with her new-fangled Butterball, prying at the button with a paring knife and muttering, "dang it, I *know* it's done."

So just when I had despaired of children ever being exposed to the consequences of their own actions, bless their hearts—they went and invented tree-surfing. A California teenager recently rode a Christmas tree towed behind an SUV, and the driver took a turn too fast and sent the surfer out on a tangent that culminated in his hitting a parked car and suffering entirely re-dundant head injuries. The driver fled. The other kids riding in the SUV said they have no idea who she was. Natural selec-tion, if given free rein, will cull every one of these people. This will cause momentary sadness, but then thanks to a variety of indulgent satellites, we'll know just where their bodies are.

Curses! Soiled Again

Recently I mused about the old manual typewriters I grew up with, and, as I'm sure it does for many of you, it put me in mind of my sex education. Not the segment of it I got from the gutter as God and, certainly, Mom intended, which was fascinating, far-fetched and turned out to be true, but the part I got from Mom. I was nine years old and she was typing out my application for summer camp. She could navigate those forms like nobody's business, barely pausing to readjust the paper so that the typing fit precisely in the little boxes. Her fingers were a blur, and then suddenly she stopped cold, turned to me and said, *Mary, do you know what menstruation is?*

Well, no. But I could tell by her expression that I probably should, and that I wasn't going to like it.

She then gave me an entirely inadequate explanation that was no explanation at all—just a description, really, and no making sense of the thing. It sounded like a perfectly horrible prospect with no real purpose (and that is, indeed, what it turned out to be), and when she finished with "do you understand?" I lied and said "yes," hoping it would end the lesson, and it did. She whipped back around to the typewriter, typed three letters in the box, and then rolled down to the next box.

There you have it: Part One of my sex education. Let's review. I cannot remember exactly how she transmitted the key information about the bleeding into the underwear region. It had to have been some delicate phrasing; we had gone years (nine, at that point) without referring to anything between anyone's legs. Or anything

that ever happened or might sometime happen in that neighborhood. Even the phrases "Number One" and "Number Two" were strictly street terminology. We used "piddle," when necessary, and that's as far as it went.

So however she put it, my memory went into the self-cleaning cycle right away, and the words are lost to history. I got the gist. Some day soon some dreadful new hygiene issue would develop in my underwear, and it was completely natural and expected, and when it happened I should come to her for Part Two, additional information and supplies. Why this revolting development should occur, as well as where babies came from and even came out of, were details I was expected to scrounge elsewhere.

So the day it happened, I went and told Mom, and she smiled and promised to "fix me up" and went to her closet, where she had a sanitary napkin all rigged up on a brand new belt for me, and—aiming for levity—she told me to come to her with any questions because she was an expert. It was excruciating. I took the item into the bathroom with me and never asked her another thing. This was just one more horrible aspect of getting older, among many that were surfacing at the time.

The next day at school I did have a momentary lift and the sense of having joined the maturity club when I asked to be marked down for a "sponge bath" in gym, but that was it for high points. Everything else about the situation sucked. The napkin felt like a mattress before it got compressed into an inadequate narrow log, and the act of walking tended to make it migrate to the rear where it wasn't really needed, and away from where it was. I developed the tactic of nonchalantly backing into the corner of a desk, as if resting, to reposition the thing, a solution that needed repeating every thirty steps or so. Various innovations improved the situation over the years, but there was really no shining it up.

In the seventies it became fashionable to celebrate anything related to being female. Restrictive underwear was discarded, sometimes publicly, pronouns were redeployed, vibrator sales were humming, and, in some quarters, it was considered liberating to celebrate one's menses as the source of some kind of mythic goddess power. Drape yourself in purple, doll up your shrine, maybe do a taste test.

I was no prude. There's photos to prove it. I tried, but you can't polish a turd into a pearl. My friend Linda, who is a mother and in whose life there was at least some point to this disgusting event, once hiked with me on beautiful Mt. Hood. Not that it wasn't a splendid day with much to be excited about, but I was startled to see her chatting away on the trail with her hand down her pants. "What are you doing?" I asked.

"I'm checking to see if I started my period," she said.

"With your *finger*?"

Linda pulled it out and examined it. "What," she said, "you haven't gone digital yet?"

The entire revolting process lurched and skidded to a halt a few years ago for me. It was forty years of pointlessness and laundry. Nothing changed my initial impression of it when I was nine. I guess Mom did a good job communicating after all.

Snow Cone Boy

"No, I'm just—I'm just trying to explain to my son, here—I'm trying to explain to him that he can't always—"

The woman at the pool shook her head as if it were full of bugs. "I mean, no, we're not in line for the bathroom."

That was the question I'd asked her. She was so wrapped up in explaining something to her son that she didn't realize she didn't need to explain it to everybody. And it shouldn't have taken much explanation for her son. One smack upside the head should have cleared it all up.

The son really, really, really wanted a snow cone. There were snow cones available right outside. All mommy needed to do was fetch him one, and, as far as he could see, problem solved.

"You're not getting a snow cone."

But he really, really, really wanted one.

"Are you hungry?"

He really wanted a snow cone.

"Because if you're hungry, we can all go home right now. We can all of us, your sisters and brother and you, we can just turn right around and go home. We can have some lunch and then we can all get in the car and come back here and then we can go swimming in the afternoon swim period."

This is the modern parenting paradigm. You negotiate by offering the child choices, and that way the child never has to feel the sting of utter refusal. First time I saw it in action, a young mother was begging her child to walk south down the street with her. The child had north in mind, and hard. Mommy took a few steps south, making wheedly noises, but her kid wasn't worried about being left behind. Sure enough, Mommy doubled back and caught up with the northbound train. "We're going this way," she sang out, pointing south. "Would you like to walk, or would you like to skip?" Skipping really hit the spot. The little girl skipped north. Man, what a skipper! Mommy had lots of time to come up with a new choice before she caught up.

It's quite a time-consuming routine. It takes a bucket of patience. The woman at the pool was hanging onto hers by a very thin thread, and the son was sawing on it with a razor-blade whine. He was *this close* to a snow cone, he felt certain.

His siblings stood by anxiously watching negotiations. They had their swimsuits on and were wrapped in towels. The pool was a few yards away. *Would he call her bluff?*

"Okay, let's go home," he said. *Yes, he would!*

The mother was completely at a loss. Her other three children were staring at her, waiting to see if they had to go back home and change and have lunch and come back in a few hours.

Presumably, the deal with offering choices is that the child will always feel a measure of control. Because he can choose, he will not feel it necessary to schedule a tantrum. Sure enough, Junior here had a measure of control. Actually, he had all of it. Mom was down to one choice, herself. Cave in, or murder him, which is still frowned upon when mothers do it, even in the blue states.

My parents were also into choices. I can't remember specifically the kinds of choices I was offered, but one of them was always "or else," always implied. If further explanation was required, it was done with the flat of the hand, which had the advantage of being quick and easy to understand. My older sister, who was smarter and more sensitive, was able to get the gist of the choice with a significantly raised parental eyebrow. Neither of us wasted any time on a tantrum, or the whiny run-up, neither of which ever bore fruit. Ever. A couple times a year I sensed that Mommy could be talked into buying a Danish at the Safeway because she wanted one too. That was about the extent of it. I didn't even try it if I didn't catch the Danish-aisle linger on the way to Dairy.

The neighbor girl used to get beaten with a switch. She had to go find the switch herself. That always had a sickening Jesus-lugging-his-own-cross aspect to it. But this wasn't considered un-usual at the time. It did have the advantage of introducing the child to the concept that life isn't fair and she can't always have what she wants. The whole idea that I should get my way, just because, never entered my head. There were people in charge in my house, and they weren't me. This seemed normal and right. My mother told me later that I was spanked at least once a day for the first two or three years of my life, until I outgrew it. I remember only two of the spankings. Those, I didn't think I had coming. Evidently, all the rest of them were right on the money. I bear no scars. And mom and dad probably never even considered murder. All in all, a fine system.

Back at the pool, Snowcone Boy sized up the situation and discov-ered he was at an advantage in the ongoing negotiations. Mom had made a tell-tale hesitation, as her other children looked up in concern, lower lips quivering. Would she really take them all home again when they were this close to getting in the pool? Homeland Security would have assessed the Constrained Exasperation Alert in the red zone. Snowcone Boy almost grinned. He saw a snow-cone in his immediate future, in exchange for agreeing not to re-turn home for lunch, plus a forfeited candy bar to be named later. Life was good.

It was Dave who had the perfect intervention idea. At 6'5" and two hundred pounds, he was just the fellow to carry it out, too. He would clap a meaty hand on the boy's shoulder, turn him around and march him off, saying, "All right, champ. Let's go meet your new mother. You've broken this one."

Did he do it? We're both still this side of the jail. But wouldn't it have been swell?

This Bud's For You

We were walking the other day through a tucked-away little alley and approaching a small knot of teenagers when the sweet smell of pot drifted our way. Smells have a way of transporting you back to very specific times in your life, and this one did, too. Unfortunately, it reminded me of a time in my life I don't remember very well, so nostalgia never really got a foothold. Still, I was favorably disposed, until we drew closer and I saw that the teenagers had become very quiet and one of them was trying on a look of dignified defiance, and I realized we were the Encroaching Old Farts. "Want me to freak them out?" Dave asked, and I said "no," but as we passed them by Dave let out: "we used to pay fifteen bucks an ounce for that." I think he's still chuckling.

It's not entirely true, of course. What we paid fifteen bucks an ounce for was similar to compost in appearance and effect, and once you'd carded out all the seeds on your LP jacket, it still took a good bit of puffing to get anywhere. The first time I tried it I was fourteen and camping out on Old Rag Mountain, far from my parental units. That's what you get when your club chaperone is a college freshman. There was no effect that time, or the time after that, but the third time, a bunch of us were driving somewhere and the light a block up ahead turned red and it seemed to take us a half hour to get up to it. "Whoa," the driver said upon reaching the intersection, and that struck all of us as high comedy. We giggled for a couple hours, or possibly a couple minutes, I'm not sure, and then we had to go get brownie hot fudge sundaes just to settle down.

Every time I noticed I was stoned, what I really noticed was that I had been stoned for the last five minutes. Time seemed to have developed a degree of elasticity. At some point, after a few years of this, my brain began to be alarmed by its own elasticity and it began to play with the idea of going completely nuts and just getting it all over with. This wasn't pleasant. I had my sanity by a thread, and I tethered it to any friend I could draft to stay put and not leave me. He or she would hang onto the thread while my brain kited around in Looneyville. After an hour or so (or possibly five minutes, I'm not sure) the threat would subside. Then, a few days later, someone would be passing around another joint, and I'd do it all over again. This continued on and off for about ten years. Why?

Well, because there were a lot of truths my generation held to be self-evident, among them that war was evil, materialism was evil, doing laundry was overrated and pot was harmless. Everyone knew these things. I regarded every single pot-induced panic attack as an anomaly. "Maybe *this* time it will be fun again," I would think. Nope. We didn't notice that we smelled, either.

Then the war folded up, immediately followed by our idealism, and we discovered how much fun money is, and we bought a lot of new toys and some really big-ass automobiles, destroyed the climate and the economy and loused everything up in general for our children. I don't know how they're able to afford the new pot, but they're welcome to it. We owe them that, at least.

Whey To Go

A struggle has been brewing between two warring factions of the Department of Agriculture, and no clear winner has emerged, except for the American consumer, who now averages one-quarter cheese by volume, and boy, is he happy.

The Department of Agriculture is interested in the promotion of good health, and its subsidiary, Dairy Management, is interested in the promotion of cheese. The dilemma arose when the agency promoting health stripped the fat out of the milk. Something needed to be done with the excess fat, and cheese ensued. The government bought it up and stockpiled it in cool caves in Missouri, to the tune of over four billion dollars' worth. Additional semi-liquid Brie deposits are thought to exist in the shale layers.

The problem was exacerbated by cow enhancement. Early cows were very different from the ones we have today, which have been engineered to be giant udders stabilized with hooves on each corner. These new bovoids are further stimulated by special lighting, in the same manner already proven effective in Las Vegas. They bob into the barns and hit the slots, ultimately resulting in yet more cheese.

I thought I knew where milk came from when I was a child. God dropped it off cold in a bottle with a cardboard tab and left it on the back porch. Later in the fifties I made acquaintance with some of the early evolutionary forms of cow at my Uncle Cliff's farm in North Dakota. Uncle Cliff maintained a small herd of terrifying black and white cows. I was small and easily stepped on, and I regarded my Uncle Cliff as a giant among men, based on his willingness to wade into the herd and slap rumps to motivate them towards the barn, and also because he was taller than my dad, which, in retrospect, was no big feat. I was able to observe milk being extracted, before it was brought to the kitchen in a bucket for the grown-ups visiting from the city to ooh and aah over. It was revolting. It was warm and creamy and had little flecks of grass floating in it, instead of cold in a bottle on the back porch, per God's previous arrangements.

Anyway, to recap, the Department of Agriculture has now been forced to contend with the excess of fat brought on by the skimming of milk as recommended by the Department of Agriculture.

Domino's Pizza was one of the first to benefit, when Dairy Management made the recommendation to discard the old recipe, in which tomato sauce product was veneered directly on the cardboard container and flecked with cheese-like nurdles, and introduce the new, in which cheese replaces the bread/cardboard layer, the tomato layer, and the layer on top primarily responsible for strip-mining the roof of your mouth. It was a hit. As the Department currently maintains, "cheese can fit into a low-fat, healthy diet," as long as it's wearing its fat pants.

Then a scientist who stockpiled pay from Dairy Management discovered that cheese could help you lose weight, and if a little cheese could do that, just think of what a lot of cheese could do. Advertising was rendered out, cheese sales soared, and when all subsequent efforts to replicate the original scientist's results failed, Dairy Management immediately withdrew its claims, after a few years and a bomb threat from the Physicians Committee for Responsible Medicine. Current research is focusing on the ability of cheese to foster hair growth and erections.

Meanwhile, cheese consumption continues to expand. We must move to protect this resource before the big corporations buy up Missouri and drill down our cheddar reserves.

Chapter 3

Science. Nature. Poop.

A Putty Good Idea
Requiem For A Biology Degree
Putting The Squeeze On Evolutionary Theory
Weed vs. Weeds
Hot Shit
Stop And Smell The Putrescine
Iguano
To Boldly Go
Traveling Light
Cool Beans

A Putty Good Idea

A homeowner not far from here burnt up his house during the recent cold snap, and all he was trying to do was warm up his chickens. That's what you get when you try to raise chickens in the city, some are clucking. But the whole disaster could have been averted had he gone all in on the urban farming. What he needed was a cow.

There is a growing appreciation for working with nature rather than at odds with it, not only because it's the right thing to do but because it's the most effective thing to do.

So in this case, when the heat lamp overheated in the chicken coop and the house was threatened, our city farmer would have been in much better shape had he thought to keep a cow handy. A man in Rogersville, Tennessee recently got all upset at his neighbor for allowing his cow to lick his house, doing $100 worth of damage, he claims. I don't know what constituted $100 worth of damage. Maybe the cow got some pieces of the man's siding going the wrong way. But for sure a well-licked house would be much better protected against fire than an unlicked one, and besides, it would be natural.

I've tried to apply the principle to my own life. We had no sooner put up an addition on our house than a flicker elected to drill a giant hole in it. It was way up on our tower, which made it hard to get at. After a few weeks the flicker abandoned his project to go perforate someone else's house, and we were left with a sizable hole which would likely collect moisture and begin to rot, forty feet up in the air. How can we apply a natural solution to this problem? I pondered the question for a while. What we needed was something that would fill the hole and prevent moisture damage, and the answer was hanging right there in front of my nose: sperm plugs.

Sperm plugs are left inside females by various copulating males in the animal kingdom, either to prevent insemination by a rival male or to prevent leakage of semen. Many species employ the sperm plug, not including humans, who have instead evolved the ability to do laundry. All that I would need to do is render the hole in question sexually appealing to one or the other of these species and nature would take care of it herself. Possible sperm-plugging candidates might include the boa constrictor, the banana slug, or the monkey. ("Why not something in the crab family," I hear you saying, and true, the spermatophores, or sperm packets, used by crabs might be a suitable patch, but one would want to go with a shore crab, with its simple ellipsoidal capsules of uniform thickness, and not your hermit crabs, whose spermatophores are complex, pedunculated structures; because who needs that drama? Also, most crabs do not care for heights.)

Boas seemed problematic. If there is a boa constrictor capable of scaling a vertical wall forty feet, I don't care to know about it. Slugs are prevalent and famously peckish; perhaps if we planted a hosta in the window, we could attract a raft of them, at least for a snack; but I tend to founder on the question of what passes for sex appeal in a slug, and am disinclined to do the research. Which brings us to the monkeys. They're clearly capable of getting up there, as we all know from that documentary about the Empire State Building. Unfortunately, we're very shy of monkeys in Oregon, although with climate change we might hope for an expansion of their range. This might take a while, though. And if we're going for those champion sperm-pluggers, the ring-tailed lemurs, which are native to Madagascar, we'd have to wait for plate tectonics to deliver us one, and that would take even longer, by which time they might not even be in the mood.

The more I think about eco-engineering the deposition of a coagulated post-coital gelatinous protein mass, the more I think: you know? Wood putty might work.

Requiem For A Biology Degree

I saw a flat dead squirrel today on the road. I can't bear to look at them when they're still gooey, but this one was as flat as a cartoon coyote. It occurred to me that it had really been quite a while since I'd seen a dead squirrel. Used to be, the city was chock-full of suicidal squirrels. As soon as I saw a squirrel dash ahead of me when I was driving, I would slow down or even stop, because it was guaranteed to double back to see if it could get under my wheels. I'd wait until it got all the way to the nearest tree before I'd drive on.

I have a theory about this. The reason squirrels are so whacked-out around cars is that they evolved to evade eagles, not Expeditions. If they run to and fro, and try to mix up the "to" and the "fro" a bit, they might escape death from the sky. I'm thinking that in a matter of forty or fifty years, the city squirrel population has finally evolved to reward the individual that just goes full-tilt in one direction. Because even though I still tend to slow down around racing squirrels, they don't seem to double back the way they used to.

It's either very urban of me, or very lazy, to make a study of dead fauna. I should be able to do better. I do have a dusty old Biology degree, by now vestigial. But you study what you can, and the dead stuff doesn't take as much stealth. So I noticed that another thing has changed. Years ago, we were awash in squashed opossums. Of late, they've been almost entirely displaced by dead raccoons. Did the raccoons eat the possums? It seems unlikely, possums being so stringy and greasy-looking and all, but raccoons eat a lot of things, so maybe they eat possums; after all, in some parts of the country, people do too. And they're huge (the raccoons, I mean, although some of the possum-eating humans can run a little large). I remember when they used to be medium-sized and cute. Now they stand there, leaning towards you, not backing away, looking at you eye to eye behind their villainous masks and rubbing their hands together like assassins. My night vision isn't that great, but the last one I saw was the size of a Volkswagen, had tusks and was swinging a tire iron. I don't remember them being so big before. That's one reason I think they've eaten the possums. Oh, sure, you hear about the natural shifting of fortunes of different species occupying the same ecological niche, with one population gaining temporary ascendancy due to variations in food availability and vulnerability to parasites. But one thing I learned in science was that the simplest and most elegant solution is often the best. So I'm sticking with the gigantic possum-eating raccoon hypothesis.

There's an impressive pile of poop under our grape trellis, all in one spot, and since I'm not out there at night checking, I don't know what has produced it. I do, however, have a field guide to poop, and I consulted it. My bookcase is a little light on literature, but I feel sort of proud of keeping a poop guide handy, and so I mentioned it to my sister, who was not especially impressed. She had a poop guide too. I think this says something about our family. For both of you still reading, possum poop is reported ("unfortunately," adds the guide) to lack distinctive qualities. Raccoon poop, it goes on, is not tapered at the ends, but is more or less broken-off. I see that as careless and lazy on the part of raccoons. The guide says raccoon and possum poop are easily mistaken one for the other, and in both cases they vary according to what is being eaten. I do not know if the poop of possum-eating raccoons is distinctive.

I do know they're up to no good. Poop should be tapered.

Putting The Squeeze On Evolutionary Theory

I am indebted to a reader for bringing the article "Why You Should Give A Square Shit About Wombats" to my attention, and where were the rest of y'all? Literally dozens of people must have known that wombats produced cubic poop and didn't tell me, but this is not a good thing to hold in. Cubic poops are the building blocks of a blog post, at the least. Add a plumb bob, a level and a vat of Febreze, and you've got yourself a domicile.

Wombat poop looks like the squared-off chunks from the larger size Tootsie Rolls of my youth. Tootsie Rolls didn't taste very good, but they were cheap and didn't taste good for a long long time, and I speculate the same could be said for wombat poop. If all goes well, we shall never know. But why, you might ask, do wombats crank out cubes in the first place?

The prevailing theory includes the observation that many animals poop to mark their territory. According to this scenario, some among the early wombattery noticed that turds with corners did not roll away, and they popped them out on rocks and logs like heads on a pike, proclaiming: *keep out, this is my space.* I would argue that this is at best a secondary reason to poop, but it has merit. I used to do the same thing with used Kleenex and toenail clippings when I had roommates. Also, since the wombat can be confident his crap will remain where he left it, he can easily find his way home. Since he snaps off 80-100 dice a day, this can get him pretty far afield.

This theory implies that without boxy poop, all the wombats in a given population trying to find their way home via the process of elimination would wind up bunched together in a ravine, or some other low spot. I see a number of problems with this. For one, I have not observed that shit in general does a lot of rolling. It's sticky. I have counted on this very property of shit over the years, as one who can only find the direction of a slope in the woods by observing which of my feet gets wet when I pee. Also, you *can* roll dice. *Especially* in craps.

It's hard to squeeze out a solid evolutionary advantage to cube-pooping. Wombats do take fourteen days to digest their food, so that suggests a certain amount of backup, and their posteriors are made of cartilage. There is much to indicate that squaring up one's poop takes a toll.

Whatever the reason, somebody has found a market in paper made of wombat poop. It is dense and fibrous, and, after all, it's already square, but I suspect that the original innovator got the idea because of the poop's stay-puttedness. "Look," our inventor said, a dim light bulb going off over his head, "it's stationary." (Yes, it should be "stationery." This is the kind of thing you get in the spell-check generation, and also explains why so many little asses are running boroughs in New York City.)

Speaking of burrows, which we almost were, that is where wombats live. They are excellent, if slow, excavators, spending a lot of time pointing downwards with their bony rears in the air. Being marsupials, they carry their young in a pouch for six to seven months, while they tell them how smart and talented they are. The kids come back later after they spend some time in the real world and discover no one else wants to buy their drawings. The pouches are installed backwards, so dirt doesn't get in them while the mama wombat digs into her burrow. This situation puts the little ones at risk of falling out when she goes back uphill, but fortunately, baby wombats are square. They don't go anywhere.

All of this is a lot to ask natural selection to account for. The alternative is to postulate that God, by the eighteenth or nineteenth day, just flang out a bony-assed fuzzy critter that carries its young in a pocket with a view of its own butt and likes to produce geometrically pleasing turds on rocks, just for the pure hell of it. I'm a science girl, but I'm going with Number Two. That's sure what I'd do.

Weed Vs. Weeds

I'm an avid gardener, but I'm not indulgent. I like to introduce my plants to adversity early on so they learn to cope. This is a tough old world, I tell them. Mommy may not always be here to protect you. Sometimes the rain won't fall, sometimes the sun won't shine, sometimes a fleet of cutworms will hack you off at the ankles. Sometimes, I warn darkly, Mommy will be too busy having a few beers and throwing darts over by the tool shed to tend to your every need.

Still, there are always a few specimens I try to keep an eye on: new citizens without the rootage to withstand drought, potted plants that whine for water or fertilizer. So when I go away for a few weeks, I try to enlist a caretaker and I try to keep it simple. Just make sure the flowerboxes get water, I explain. You might want to check on this little guy over here, I point out. He's a recent transplant. But generally I expect to entertain a few losses.

I needn't have fretted. In the two weeks since we'd been gone, the topiary frog looked ready to leap. The ears of corn met the elephant's eye. The cherry tomatoes lit out for the territories, and the heirlooms sent a posse out after them. The strawberries were studying a plat for a new development and negotiating with the diascia for open space. Peppers popped. Zauschnerias split up into gangs and roughed up the other ground covers.

The squash, showing deference to the seniority of the tomatoes on the east side, galloped to the west and made for a patch of marigolds. The toad lilies were hoppy. Buzz was building for the Shakespeare

Festival on the north side, with the nicotiana and datura duking it out for the part of Oberon, King of the Fairies. The little eyringium, which had knocked the Puck audition out of the park, regarded impassively. Encouraged, the new pomegranate got together with a few reticent players in the aster family and set up a chapter of Toastmasters International, gaining confidence with every performance.

The phlox stood up and cheered as the helianthums busted out into a chorus of *Didn't It Rain, Oh My Lord, Didn't It Rain*. The caryopteris shot up two feet to see what the commotion was. The gloriosa daisy shot up three, to see over the caryopteris. The scrub jays, who had started a book group, were unperturbed. As is the case in most book groups, nothing much got read; they were basically in it for the blueberry nosh.

The hummingbirds did one round each on the fuchsias and then had to go lie down for a while; I don't where the sofa, barely visible under the blue hosta, came from. The star jasmine not only made it to the bottom rung of the new trellis, but went condo on a nearby rogue asparagus plant. The lemon cucumber exhausted its vertical possibilities and shot out over the zinnias. The hibiscus is treating it as a hostage situation.

The only plant that looks to be a little worse for wear is a handsome but dissolute penstemon, which had always been known to drink too much, given the opportunity, and was found staggering over the ground. It will probably recover, given the chance to dry out, and now that I'm back in charge, that's a chance it's likely to get.

As for the weeds, half appeared to have been dispatched and the rest terrified. A particularly tenacious colony of oxalis between the stepping-stones had been completely rooted out, possibly with a spoon and tweezers, and all the thistle seeds have blown away, bearing tales of a holocaust.

So this is what a garden looks like when it gets every little thing it wants. All it ever needed was to be left for a few weeks in the custody of a nice woman with a lot of time on her hands. And a pretty good stash of pot.

Hot Shit

I just read this. Apparently if humans go in for radiation treatment on their thyroid glands, they are instantly sent home, free on their own recognizance, which is legal for "out on their fanny." The reason this is odd is that if your cat goes in for the exact same procedure, she is quarantined for three or four days while her radioactivity wears off. And if anything, your average human is much bigger and more radioactive than any cat, except the jug-butt one down the street that probably has a thyroid the size of a bagel. The real reason they punt out the human patients is it costs five thousand dollars an hour to be housed in a hospital, even if you're in self-wiping condition, and the insurance companies would rather take their chances sending you home on the bus where most of the other passengers are probably uninsured.

They're pretty strict about the cats. I sent my cat Larry in for the procedure after I made her promise to live another three years. It's expensive. It was just under a thousand bucks at the time, and only available in two places in the whole state. I felt lucky we were only twenty miles away from the facility. I imagined the radiation involved a huge machine and the cat would be splayed out and duct-taped down and passed through it while it buzzed and bonged and Dr. House smirked at her from the observation room. So when I came in the door and traded my boxed kitty for a sheaf of papers to fill out, and she was whisked away, I asked when the procedure would be done. "They probably already did it," the receptionist said.

Huh?

"It's just an injection of radioactive iodine," she said. "It goes straight to the thyroid gland, zap zap." Nine hundred and some dollars for an injection? "And the boarding," she pointed out.

Boarding means Larry is in a little cage for three days with a camera trained on her so that we could visit her from home via our computer. We studied the grainy image for days. It was the quality of a convenience store security camera. "That's her, all right," Dave said. "She isn't moving."

"She's *asleep*," I said, hoping that was what she was. The second day a tabby came in wearing a ski mask and made off with her kibble.

They're serious about the radiation thing. When I picked her up, I was given a list of instructions. Her bodily waste was to be considered highly toxic for a month. We got a special bag of lead-pellet litter and sturdy bags and two-foot tongs and a prayer book. Everything was to be double-bagged for a month and put directly in the garbage can outside. We were to avoid getting close for a week—no lap-sitting. It was unnerving. I listened for a hum from the cat and reminded myself she'd always had green eyes.

Disaster struck immediately. The combination of being shot up and kenneled for days and crated and put in a *car* unraveled Larry's last tether to sanity. When we pulled onto the freeway, she suddenly cut loose with three days of liquefied radioactive poop. The crate looked like something had blown up in the microwave and the stench could have dropped a moose. Larry kept up a siren yowl while I drove home doing 85 mph with my head out the window, mostly in my lane, and once home I held the crate out as far from my body as I could and dropped her on the mudroom floor, still yowling, and phoned the clinic in a panic. "My cat, crate, and parts of my car are *covered in radioactive shit* and *I'm not supposed to touch her*. What do I do? Put her in the alley and open the hydrant?"

They were very calm and instructed me to wash the cat in the sink and clean everything up and everything would be fine, by which they meant the statute of limitations on their liability would expire before I do. I suppose there was nothing else to suggest.

I don't see why people don't get the same treatment. I wouldn't want a camera trained on me at all times, because I'd never get my nose picked, but all kinds of people are happy to, and they end up on magazine covers and the whole country knows them by first name. The people defending the release of radioactive humans from the hospital like to claim that people can be trusted to follow instructions regarding their own effluent and maintain a proper distance from others, which is not true. Many adults of my acquaintance are capable of filling their shorts at any time. And if Dave came home radioactive and was told to stay several feet away from me, he would rise from his chair and lurch towards me all tilty with his arms out and a zombie leer, just to see me scream and run away. He could do this all week, and never tire of it. This is a fact.

Stop And Smell The Putrescine

It's June, and outside in the south garden is the unmistakable reek of a whompingly dead animal. Something large. It always makes me want to go out there and cut one.

There's no trouble locating the offending object, even if you didn't have all those flies to follow. It's in the same place every year. Dracunculus vulgaris is a plant magnificent in leaf and flower, and it's just the sort of thing you'd want front and center on your dining room table, if only it didn't smell like extract of dead possum. It's a gigantic flower, the sort referred to by garden-design types as "architectural." Unfortunately the building it most calls to mind is the slaughterhouse. I did cut one once, early in the morning before it had really expressed itself, and then I went off to work. I think I had forgotten its hidden talents, and I just thought it made quite a statement. Dave had some people over later and they all got the statement loud and clear. I got in trouble.

This particular plant was here when we moved in thirty years ago, and it took a while to discover its properties. The bloom lasts but a few days and the stink just one. It took a few years just to realize that we *didn't* have a vat of dead possums out there. And we'd gotten used to the vultures. About twenty-five years into our relationship with this plant, it started putting out little seedlings, and I've taken to repotting them and giving them to my friends. At least once a year, I know they'll be thinking of me.

I suppose it's just species-ist of me, but I do tend to look down on flies for being attracted to poop and dead things. I understand how the system works, but it just seems wrong. I guess everything is just a matter of taste, but it seems like you really have to draw the line somewhere. I actually draw it just in front of oysters.

There's already a minor enterprise afoot in sending a bouquet of dead roses to people with whom you're quarreling, and I think someone is missing a bet with this flower. You could have one potted up and sent to someone just as it's beginning to unfurl. Someone like, oh, your congressman. "Thanks for all your good efforts on behalf of the private insurance industry," the note might say. Or, "Just a little appreciation for your work in keeping the country safe for heterosexuals." Your congressman will put the magnificent flower in the front office and smile. Until tomorrow.

Iguano

You've probably heard the terrible news about Daniel Bennett and his missing lizard feces. Mr. Bennett had saved over five years' worth of the feces of Philippine Butaan lizards and then Leeds University went and lost it. I know just how he feels. I lose shit all the time. Things are constantly going missing. Dave takes a much darker and more accusatory view of this phenomenon than I do; I tend to start sentences with "have you seen the..." while Dave says "what did *you* do with the..." but neither one of us ever figures out who did the losing, because we never find anything.

Poor Daniel Bennett was nearly through with his doctoral thesis on the lizard, variously described (in the article) as "shy" and "extinct," which is just an extreme form of shy. He was studying the shit in lieu of disturbing the actual lizards, theoretical or otherwise, which is delicate of him. This leads me to conclude that he is not only a considerate man but a very serious scientist, probably avant-garde as zoologists go, because what he's doing is a lot like research into particle physics. Particle physics is the study of things that might not even exist, so if particle physicists are wrong about anything, no one will ever know. That's part of what gives particle physicists their reputation for smarts. What they like to do is send their particles whizzing through colliders at insane speeds, and sometimes something goes "poink" and that, there, is your—well, no, not your quark *per se*, but evidence that your quark has been in the area. In other words, the most brilliant scientists in the world spend their time poking through quark shit. It's a living.

The university was profoundly sorry it had lost Mr. Bennett's sack of academic material, all seventy-seven pounds of it, but in its

defense it noted that the sack was not labeled. It had been there for upwards of five years, and someone finally took the initiative to dispose of it, greatly upsetting Mr. Bennett. It's sort of like the time I put Dave's golf clubs in a yard sale when he hadn't touched them in ten years and then *all of a sudden* they turned out to have been the key to happiness. I'm sure if the 77-pound sack had been properly labeled ("shit"), no one would have dreamed of throwing it away.

To Boldly Go

I wasn't quite in Junior High when John Glenn, who lived across the street from the school, blasted into space, but I was like all children of the time who thrilled to the venture and the possibility of landing a man on the moon, and wondered how they went potty. Number Two was always number one in our minds, and it was hard to suppress visions of tumbling turds in the spacecraft and the possible variations on dodge-ball that might ensue. Well, we were children. Sadly, it doesn't get much more sophisticated when you grow up.

In fact it puts me in mind of a particular morning in the post office, where I worked, when the boss came on the intercom with an announcement. The sewer workers had the lines open right outside our building and there had been a request that we refrain from using the toilets to do anything important if we could possibly help it. Well, you haven't seen a group of workers pull together and strain for a common purpose like that in your life. Just the thought that someone would be in a position to admire our interpretive renditions of last night's burritos was enough to inspire a regular flotilla past the sewer workers, special delivery, flushed with pride.

Postal workers may be a special subset of humanity, but everyone wonders how the astronauts cope. And it has proved vexing even for rocket scientists. Even Number One is troublesome. Each astronaut is equipped with his own funnel, in one of three sizes, the smallest of which, in the interest of maintaining morale, is called "large." Female astronauts would seem to be at a bit of a disadvantage, and that is indeed so, but they were marginally better off when it came to Number Two. The astronauts contemplating a boom-boom were required to use individual fecal bags which they taped to their

buttocks and then ripped off. Hairlessness was to one's benefit. Shortly before I blacked out, I learned that the bags, once removed, required kneading.

All this was ameliorated with the invention of the space toilet. The main problem with the process of elimination in space is, um, separation. I had not properly appreciated the role of gravity in disconnecting ourselves from our waste materials. I had always thought we bring a certain amount of pressure to bear, especially sometimes, but it actually takes the entire mass of the planet to finish the job. Lacking that, we can remain attached to our effluent. It does shine a new light on Neil Armstrong's famous moonwalk, already a cheerful, bouncy affair, which would only be jollied up by a set of dancing dingleberries, don't you think? Fortunately, our astronauts do not need to float about the space station trailing a string of sausages. All that is required is some negative pressure, a.k.a. suction. Negative pressure for the separation of urine from men is no doubt a finely calibrated thing. Too little, no separation; too much, no urine. They probably tested for months.

Merging a toilet with a vacuum was fraught at first. Four out of five astronauts were unhappy with the beater bar. And maneuvering to the toilet in space takes practice. Flatulence can send an astronaut tumbling through the air; on Bean Night, it could even lead to head injuries. The toilet itself is a hole only four inches wide, and positioning is vital. The astronaut must center himself and clamp himself down with handles over the thighs (see "flatulence," above). The fecal matter is stored in a cylinder with what is called "unlimited storage capacity," which is another name for space. It is periodically expelled from the craft and eventually returns to earth, where what doesn't burn out during re-entry—and who among us hasn't experienced *that*—rains down mainly on the offices of Fox News, which has the most efficient dispersal mechanism.

The collected urine, on the other hand, is purified to the point of being potable, a process which led directly to the invention of Tang.

All of this required a lot of testing before it was put into place. The only place to test weightlessness on earth is the Vomit Comet, an airplane that in the course of a steep parabolic flight pattern delivers the sensation of weightlessness for about 25 seconds. In order to test their toilet, NASA needed to come up with volunteers who could pop a doot in that amount of time.

No one in our household will be represented, I know that. The second the Vomit Comet takes off I will have suffered a premature evacuation. And Dave, who prides himself on his abilities in this department and loves thrill rides to boot, will be turned away at the door when they see him lumbering up with a stack of magazines.

Traveling Light

Nippon Airways has announced a new program of encouraging their passengers to use the toilet before boarding aircraft. This simple step was calculated to save enough weight and fuel to reduce the airline's carbon emissions. (An uptick in methane gas production was not factored in, so it may be a wash for the climate as a whole.) So far the program is voluntary, but I think they'll get a lot of cooperation. The Japanese have been jammed in together for so long that they have developed an admirable sense of community. We're way more lone-ranger here in America and I suspect such a request would cause considerable strain. Nobody tells *us* what to do.

The only viable approach an American airline could take would be to appeal to our sense of competitiveness. They could set it up like a tournament, double-elimination of course; maybe offer t-shirts to the winners ("I lost weight—Ask me how!"). I know I'd never be in the running because I don't perform well under pressure. There I'd be, worrying not only that I packed too much shit, but that my shit was too packed.

My suspicions about the obstinacy of Americans were confirmed when I went online to read about the airline's new policy, and found the article followed by a thread of startlingly angry comments. These were all courtesy of the global-warming denial set, who suffer from a condition that appears on the same chromosome as poor grammar and incivility. It's hard for me to imagine getting that worked up about such a simple, straightforward potty request, but this was a crew all ready to hit the town halls yelling "hell, no, we won't go." I don't know what you can say about a

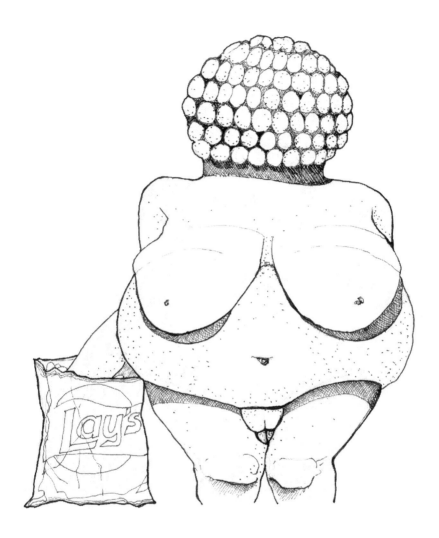

group that regards constipation as a thoughtful response to the threat of Climate Change Scolding. Almost anything passes as a movement these days, I guess. Well, they're welcome to it. They may not be backed up by science, but at least they're backed up.

My only issue with all of this is that it legitimizes an activity around this house that I had been trying to ignore for some time. Dave has such an enthusiastic metabolism that he likes to monitor it. When he's feeling especially productive, he likes to weigh himself before and after taking a dump. I tend to be dismissive about this little hobby but that's because I, personally, unlike some people I know, have never bounded out of the bathroom (with a new spring in my step) and announced that I just lost seven pounds in three minutes. And if I had, I would have gained it all back by somehow coming into contact with a vapor of potato chip molecules. Those of us who are put together like an ancient stone-age fertility fetish have missed our glory time by several thousands of years, and we can be cranky about it.

The only way I can see this working out for me is at the doctor's office, where I am already in the habit of subtracting a certain number of pounds from what their scale says based on a universal standard (one pound per clothing item, including underwear, and two pounds per shoe). Now, inspired by Nippon Airways, I can also knock off several pounds for Digested Items In Progress. It doesn't really make sense that I'd prefer to think I was 125 pounds and full of shit, rather than 134, but I do. I'll be needing an aisle seat, please.

Cool Beans

One wonders how some foods were discovered. Who was the first to defy the conventional wisdom that tomatoes were poisonous and say, "death be damned, it just isn't pizza without it?" What lovesick sailor slapped a tongue on the first oyster? Whoever had the gumption to saw into the first chicken-fried steak? Well, two out of three ain't bad.

We have a pretty good idea how the first batch of Kopi Luwak, or Civet Coffee, came about, however. Civet coffee is made from coffee beans that have passed through the digestive tract of a small mammal called the Asian Palm Civet. All the way through. The civet naturally prefers the very finest, sweetest beans at the very pinnacle of ripeness. Coffee bean farmers, who maintain a dicey profit margin as it is, naturally detest the civet. After attempts to interest the public in Fried-Civet-On-A-Stick fell flat, someone noticed that the coffee beans survived the trip through the mammals virtually intact, and thought: hmm. Let's brew some of this up and serve it to some obnoxious rich guy down at the hotel.

It was a hit. The coffee was proclaimed the richest and most flavorful in the world, "almost syrupy, thick, with a hint of chocolate." Some elements of the civets' digestive systems removed the bitterness from the beans and kicked in that certain something extra, which was not chocolate. "How are we going to sell this crap?" wondered the plantation owners, trailing a stick through clumps of civet poop, but that, of course, is the time-honored job of Marketing. And people were inclined to pay through the nose for the coffee. Good thing, too, because the gathering of fecally enhanced beans is very labor-intensive, as is the preparation of the beans (described as including a very, very, very thorough washing). Civet Coffee sells for upwards of $99 a cup in London. Before you can say "Chock Full O' Doots," a new market was born.

Initially, only a few of the smaller coffee farmers collected the clumps of fecal matter, considering it their civet doody. Retrieval of the poop is a time-consuming process in the wild, where, according to Wikipedia, "a civet would defecate as a means to mark its territory." [Scientific aside: this is not the primary reason the civet defecates. And if the civet is fastidious enough to poop outside his living room, he is not necessarily "marking his territory," although I suppose it comes down to the same thing.] Eventually, farmers took to keeping civets on a short leash, and doot collection was simplified.

I do not know whether the coffee is as delightful as it is made out to be. I do know that there is a certain set of humans who are willing to pay $500 for something they wouldn't drop five bucks on. Somewhere in Asia today some man is forking over suitcases of cash for a vial of powdered tiger penis to get the same effect he could have gotten with a two-dollar porn video.

Fast on the heels of the genuine civet poop coffee market's success comes the effort to produce imitation civet poop coffee. "True civet-poop taste without the civet," says Marketing, and indeed there has been some success in replicating the civet's digestive enzyme complement and treating beans with it. The demand is expected to grow due to the increasing scarcity of the civet population, in large part because most of the larger coffee plantation owners would still rather kill civets than scoop poop. A lab in Vietnam got the jump on its competitors in producing simulated civet coffee during the Great Civet Constipation Epidemic of '98. Their efforts were the primary engine behind the proliferation of Grunt 'N' Grind franchises all over southeast Asia. Real or imitation, however, civet coffee is good to the last dropping.

Chapter 4

What In Tarnation

Butt Load
The Electronic Leash
Look Out! It's A Cycle Path!
Toot! Toot! All Aboard The Colonoscopy Bus!
Things That Drop Out Of The Sky
Just Breathe Normally
Staying Up For The Game
To Form A More Fabulous Union
Where Does The Dime Go?
Ticketmonster

Butt Load

I'm foggy about measurements. I can never remember how far a farthing can go, or how furry a furlong is. And now I've forgotten how many units are in a butt load.

This is important, because we are planning a party of sorts; a cheerful wake, really, a celebration of life, and we don't know how many people to expect. There's a core group of us who are putting this thing together. Dave and I volunteered our house. Among the chores farmed out to others was organizing and keeping track of the RSVPs so we'd know how much food to provide. Even though invitations were sent out with RSVP prominently printed on them, we didn't get much of a response. There's a whole group of people out there who can confidently go on and on about RSS and URLs and ISPs and HTML and whatnot, but when hit with an RSVP they go all stupid on you. It's as though it's in another language. Which it is, of course, so our friends put out a follow-up reminder which spelled out the obligation a little more clearly. Evidently this worked pretty well, because when we inquired about how many people were coming, we got the following advisory: "hang on to your hats, there's going to be a butt load of people coming."

Most places in the world have gone with the metric system, which is the most sensible system, but here in America we've stuck by our old measurements. Having custody of an archaic system makes us feel as though we're members of a special club. Foreigners might have trouble understanding it, which also thrills us, and we never go anywhere, so we don't have to feel dumb. There's just something satisfying about calculating your own height in units which once corresponded to the length of a portion of the King's anatomy—let's say his foot, to be on the safe side. And the tradition of using what are, at heart, entirely arbitrary units of measurement goes back to biblical times. Let us not forget how important it was for Noah to get his ark up to specifications, using the correct proportions of rods and cones, so there'd be room enough for the cubits. The cubits must have been the same sex, because you hardly ever see them anymore.

But back to the butt load of people who will be coming to our house. We need to rent plates and wine glasses, so I guess we can just go to the rental place and ask for a butt load of each; we can buy two butt loads of beer, and a half butt load of wine, and we should be good to go. We've got the place spiffed up, and even remembered to make sure there was plenty of toilet paper on hand. I don't know what made us think of that.

Our friend Tom, whose life we're celebrating, was living in rural France with his wife Linda, who is still there, and who thus can't make it to the party in his honor. Among her other charms, she keeps a gracious home and hearth and would know just what to do if a butt load of people were to show up at her house. Although, in our defense, I think a metric butt load is a little smaller.

The Electronic Leash

It has recently come to my attention that you can have your own daughter chipped like a wayward terrier, and thus avoid all worry in life. The chipping can be done without surgery, since your daughter is never separated from her cell phone. It's called a Family Locator App and it's so accurate you can call in a missile strike on the little darling. How cool is that? I learned this through a TV ad in which a mother watches her teenage daughter recede into the distance down a shopping mall escalator—now ten, now twenty feet away—while a map floats over her head. The mother has the look of fondness and bitten-lip concern appropriate to a woman watching her only child board the Mayflower on the way to the New World. How much calmer would our old-world matron have been if, at any time, she could have ascertained her daughter's whereabouts within inches! "Forsooth, she's leaving the Macy's perfume counter," our bereft mother would report, "and heading over to Cinnabon."

It's hard to imagine our modern mother getting much of anything done with this much technology. Already she can't go fifteen minutes without checking Facebook to find out if Lulu is still grumpy and needs coffee, or if Ryan has decided to get his tires rotated after all. Tracking one's own progeny as well would seem to be a full-time occupation. When we took our cat Larry in for radiation treatments and could go online to watch the Cat-Cam focused on her kennel, that's all we did. "Still asleep," we'd report to each other, several times an hour. It's not healthy.

I have a sneaking suspicion that these new abilities actually increase worry. I'm certain it would have taken years off my own mother's

life if she had been able to know where I was all the time. Secrecy and deception, done right, can be loving gestures.

Dave and I are still phoneless and quite comfortable being lost. Even in the grocery store, I can't call him in Dairy to tell him I'm in the meat aisle. We have no idea where the other is unless we run into each other. People don't know how we can stand it, but we're used to it. Believe it or not, that's the way it was for everybody not all that long ago. There are some benefits to getting lost. We'd have never seen the entire north half of Vancouver Island if it were not for Dave and his remarkably inventive sense of direction.

No one else really knows where we are at any given time either. It's like we're invisible. I do recognize that this is an illusion. In reality, we're living in a world where scientists are able to track penguin populations by seeing their rust-colored poop on the snow from space. So finding me should be a snap.

I'm always leaving my shit all over the place.

Look Out! It's A Cycle Path!

Well, you have to go back to physics class to truly understand bike lanes. Not the comprehensible kind of Newtonian physics from your childhood, either, but the newer bits, the kind that if you claim to understand it, it proves you don't. When I was a child, science was a snap. We just had those neat little atoms all over the place. The Russians had launched a little satellite, a crappy one by today's standards, and suddenly everything was all about the atom. You saw pictures of them everywhere. Nuclei with electrons whizzing predictably about them. They were so tidy. Tennis ball in the center, ping pong balls on wire hoops.

Then it turned out that you couldn't *really* represent the atom with a tennis ball and wire hoops after all. The electrons didn't *really* travel on wire hoops. All that the purported path of the electron could represent was the probability that the electron would be right about *there*, or maybe in the next block, or halfway through the world, or sometime next week. But only if you weren't looking at it. I believe that sums up the new physics. It's not tidy at all.

But it does help to understand bike lanes.

A painted bike lane represents the probability that a bike will be encountered somewhere in its vicinity, or possibly two lanes over, or parked in the garage, or on your windshield. It just narrows things down a little.

Count me in favor of bike lanes. As a biker, I find them at least symbolic of some sort of bicycle legitimacy on the road. They're as effective at keeping me in one piece as my marching sign ("Whoa, Cowboy!") was in keeping us out of war in Iraq, but at least they're something. My preference would be for bike paths that looked more like the broad top of the Great Wall of China, with the automobile traffic dashing about below. As it is, it's still too easy to imagine ending up as a damp smear in the bike lane, surrounded by medics with spatulas and baggies.

For instance, in one high-traffic area on the approach to the Lloyd Center Mall here in Portland, the bike lane ambles peaceably on the far right and then vanishes abruptly, only to reappear one lane over, a transition marked by a faint line of hyphens. "Look, Harold, hyphens," a passenger might say to a driver, and Harold would query "hyphens?" just before hearing a *thwack* and turning his windshield wipers on high. We bikers negotiate these transitions, cringing and praying: be nice. Be sober. Be *looking*. And then we pedal on, cars whizzing by to our left and our right, secure in our bike lanes and thinking: You can't hurt me. I'm enclosed by *road stripes*.

The road to the Lloyd Center might be paved with good intentions, but it's still hell.

Toot! Toot! All Aboard The Colonoscopy Bus!

There's something positively electrifying about being with people who are all in one place for a common purpose, bursting with pent-up energy. Picture a starting line for a race. A roomful of kindergartners, waving their hands in the air to be picked. A colonoscopy clinic waiting room.

The waiting room is filled with patients and their designated drivers, so every other person is seated on the edge of his or her chair, clenched with something like excitement, accompanied by a dour companion, who is reading a magazine and breathing shallowly. There is a restroom just a few feet away. This is a good thing. This is a bad thing.

The atmosphere is very like that inside an airplane carrying first-time skydivers, everyone facing forward, maintaining focus. In some very specific respects, it's probably identical.

I was thinking about this when I read about the mammogram bus in central Oregon. Health care can be a little hit-or-miss in rural areas, and many women find it onerous to cram in an appointment, as it were, for a mammogram when they have to travel so far to get one. So the Asher Community Health Center in Fossil, Oregon arranged to pick these women up and take them to Bend to get their x-rays, and work in a spa treatment and a shopping expedition along with it. It's almost a party atmosphere on the bus, with everyone anticipating a day of getting things permed, polished, painted, purchased, and pancaked. It's dang near jolly.

And I couldn't help but think that if it works for women needing mammograms, maybe it can work for colonoscopy patients, too.

There are probably a few logistics problems to be worked out. The preparation for a mammogram consists of making an appointment and not applying deodorant. The preparation for colonoscopy is a bit more detailed, and leads to a general sense of urgency. So it would have to be part bus, part ambulance. Call it a "flatulance." The siren could be a lot of fun. The bus would require some retrofitting: plastic seat covers would be a good idea, and some sort of hose apparatus might have to be developed which could link individuals into the exhaust system. But a good engineer might be able to make the whole thing pencil out. Rigged up properly, fuel expenses should be close to nil. It should make a dent in the tailgating problem, too.

Things That Drop Out Of The Sky

It was getting on the middle of August, time for the annual Perseids meteor shower. Dave and I are always holding out hope for a celestial doozy, something you could read the newspaper by, something just this side of a war zone. The way I see it, a person's got to die some time, and there are a lot worse ways to go about it than to be hailed on by flaming space rocks. We bring our best attitudes, lying in the lawn chairs, pointing our marshmallows towards the sky. Hey, optimism is free. But although Portland, Oregon is a pretty terrific city, it's still a city, and if one is to really appreciate a meteor shower, it's best to go a little ways out of town.

So we went to Maine.

Sadly, this involved air travel. Air travel can produce horrors for even the most intrepid traveler, and I am notably trepid. Even my most routine trips have a way of going sideways. All we had to do in this case was get ourselves deposited in Boston and we would be scooped up and carried off by loving friends with cars, brains, and everything. We would be ferried about without a care. Linda and Walter would take care of everything. Just *get to Boston*.

Just last year, Dave and I had attempted to fly to Portland, Maine, where Linda and Walter were planning to retrieve us. At that time, they probably were unaware of our unique proclivity for disaster, and were merrily on their way to fetch us when we woke up on the floor of the LaGuardia airport, in the wrong gate, having missed our connecting flight to Maine by a good hour. Not many people with a five-hour layover miss their connecting flights. Not many people can fall asleep on the floor at LaGuardia. Not many square feet of floor at LaGuardia are devoid of bird poop.

We had a crumpled piece of paper with Linder and Walter's cell numbers on it and frantically threw quarters into a phone at the airport, which hoovered them up like a slot machine. The poor phone had not seen action in years and was clearly starving to death. It balked and barked and finally held onto a tenuous connection long enough for us to reach our friends and save them another hour of driving. One much-later flight, a taxi ride, a stint on Greyhound and about twelve hours later, we were scooped up at Boston and all of us tried beerily to put the day behind us.

So on this occasion Walter reviewed the arrangements by e-mail and asked, in a hopeless postscript, if we had somehow managed to acquire our own cell phones in the intervening year. (Even in e-mail his query had a certain bleakness to it, as though he were a musician on the Titanic examining the bass fiddle for buoyancy.) Of course, we hadn't.

We boarded the plane without incident, set up shop in 27B and 27C, and peered nervously at the passengers coming up the aisle. And there, lurching towards us straight out of a Gahan Wilson cartoon, wide, squid-eyed, and unhinged, was the proud tenant of seat 27A, who wedged himself in and began to expand. It was only two hours to Salt Lake City, not so very long a time to sit with my shoulders bunched up under my ears. On the next leg, however, I was delighted to discover that the window seat was occupied by a small woman, neat and narrow, who slotted herself into the seat with enough room left over for her entire aura, and who smelled like nothing at all. Ah! There she sat, just she and her romping little rhinovirus, which she presented in aerosol form for the next four hours.

Boston. Just make it to Boston. I'm familiar enough with Logan Airport to know that it always looks like the plane's going in the water, so that wasn't going to throw me. The sky was clear as we began our descent, right on time. There wasn't a cloud in it, except one really turgid one right on the runway, looking like something the tarmac burped up all on its own. The plane abruptly plunged into darkness and when the runway finally appeared, about ten yards below, it was not the section of runway the pilot had in mind. The engines roared and the plane clambered back up to the sky and headed away. After a few minutes the pilot chimed on, cheery. "Well, folks," he began predictably, "that little cloud back there wanted to give us a little trouble, so the tower has given us leave to circle around for a little while until it clears up. But don't worry—we'll get you folks back on the ground in another five minutes, one way or the other."

"Another five minutes" does not actually mean the five minutes coming right up, but rather a whole different five-minutes about an hour into the future. Also? There's only *one* way I'm interested in getting back on the ground. Not the other.

Just Breathe Normally

Some people just like to get upset. I still recall a letter to the editor I read a few years back, written by a woman who was much affronted by a local call to the citizenry to conserve water during a drought. Why should *she* be expected to let her pansies dry out, the good woman wanted to know, when examples of waste were to be seen all over? At the airport, for instance—she went on—where she had recently visited the women's restroom, equipped with an automatic flush mechanism. "My movements inside the stall triggered multiple flushes," she huffed. Well, honey. Sometimes, if you have enough movements, you're going to want those extra flushes.

I suspect even people who are not normally given to upset do get tested at the airport. Tempers flare, babies squall, service is not what we think it should be. I believe much of the anger is simply a result of unrealistic expectations. If we readjust our outlook to reflect reality, we'd be much the better for it. I have assembled a short guide to familiar airline terms in hopes that the public will benefit:

"Departure." This refers to the time the jet rolls a few dozen yards out onto the tarmac and parks.

"Full Upright Position." Same as reclined position.

"Pre-boarding." This is not the time before people board. This is the time when people board who are not you.

"Place the mask over your mouth and nose and breathe normally." Don't worry about it. No one will be expecting you to breathe normally.

"Gate B-2." Gate C-28. Hope you've got your sneakers on.

"Welcome to Phoenix." She means Welcome to Portland, although, given your personal history of spectacular travel errors, you are to be excused if you tumble into a panic.

"We would like to make your trip as pleasant as possible." As pleasant as possible is Totally Schnockered In First Class. Back in 27-C, look for peanuts and a blankie.

"Pillow." This is actually a large sanitary napkin.

"A pleasant stay in Cincinnati, or wherever your final destination is taking you." I have no idea what this means.

I hope this guide is helpful to the flying public, and would furthermore like to offer a little travel advice to some of my fellow passengers. If you get in the habit of blowing your nose instead of snorking it all back into your face, you won't have to repeatedly rattle that pile-up in your throat later on. Thank you.

Staying Up For The Game

The World Series got me parked in front of a TV again, which is good, because I'd been falling behind in my pharmaceutical ad consumption. I can't always tell what the pharmaceuticals do, but that doesn't mean I don't need them. I loved the one a few years back about the little blue pill you can take that sharpens up your athletic ability. Before the pill, the fellow couldn't hit the broad side of a barn with a football, but afterwards, man, he was just poking that baby right through the center of a swinging tire, just *drilling* it, wham wham wham. *Hell* of a pill.

So they have to mention all the side effects, too, which is how we've all learned that four hours is about the limit for having an erection, after which you should see your doctor. I don't think they mean eighteen-year-olds, who should see somebody else. The first hour of the erection is the one you're interested in, the second and third hours are for display purposes only, and then you're just sort of counting down the last hour with your doctor on speed dial. Of course, you're not going to be able to just pop in on your doctor, so you'll have to go to the emergency room. I'm thinking there is probably a way to make a grand entrance into the ER that will get you right at the head of the line and into a private room in front of the gunshot wounds and heart attacks.

They don't say what the doctor is going to do about it. The problem, as I see it, is that there is too much blood in one place, and it needs to be encouraged to go somewhere it's in short supply, such as the brain. The four-hour erection happens when the brain feels neglected and goes into a complete pout. "Don't bother sending

any of that blood back up here," the brain sniffs. "I still have no idea what you were talking about with that betting system that's guaranteed to beat the casino. As far as I'm concerned, you're on your own, Big Boy, and God forbid you should read me a little Jane Austen once in a while."

I personally do not have much of a grip on the concept of the four-hour erection. I got my windshield wipers stuck in the "up" position once, and it just turned out to be a matter of loosening the nuts. But I do remember a particularly obstreperous Jeep from my early days as a letter carrier that might shed some light on this condition. It was hell getting that Jeep to start. You had to pump it for a half hour. Once it finally got going, it had an idle set to about 8,000 RPMs, and you drove it standing on the brake. Darn thing wouldn't shut off, either. You could turn it off, take the key out, walk away, and it would still be going when you came back five minutes later. What we figured out how to do was to cut the engine when it was still in drive, stomp on the gas, and then it would backfire like mad and shudder to a halt. It's worth a shot for the four-hour erection, too. So that's *cut it, stomp on it and plug up your ears*. I'm pretty confident about this suggestion because it's not my penis.

There's a lot of good free advice on those ads about when you should see your doctor. I generally keep my own counsel. I had some little totally unauthorized thing growing inside of me once that was supposed to be harmless, but which had begun to slouch against my bladder to the point that—under certain conditions—it sort of clamped down on my urine flow. I was on the horn about that to my doctor right away, and mentioned the problem, right after asking if Crestor, Spiriva, Prevacid, Levitra, Rituxan, Aredium, Actonel or Evista was right for me. She told me that it was probably all right as long as urine was still coming out, but if it shut off completely, I should get in to the hospital right away. No, really? Let me jot that down.

To Form A More Fabulous Union

I've had occasion to revisit my earlier quandary about the raccoons and the possums. We used to have possums, now we have raccoons. I have a new theory as to why. Possibly the raccoons evicted the possums from the yard until they agree to quit hanging by the tail. Raccoons couldn't hang from their tails if they tried, but the very idea of it makes them all squirmy. From the raccoons' point of view, it simply can't be borne.

I'm basing this hypothesis on the news today that Vermont is all in an uproar again over gay marriage. They've had legal civil unions there for nine years, and evidently a whole lot of Vermonters haven't gotten used to it. Maybe they don't get out much. This week the state is considering a bill that would allow same-sex marriage. Protesters are converging on the Capitol with signs reading "Marriage—A Mother and Father For Every Child." When Dave and I got married, we were unaware that procreation was required. It isn't something we'd had in mind. At first, people asked us when we were going to have children. That line of inquiry started to peter out when we told them we'd been to a genetic counselor and found out that there was just too much risk the child would end up something like us. And *no one* asked us anymore after Dave started explaining that you couldn't make babies with spit. Aaaany-hoo.

I guess we'll have to forgo travel to Vermont in case they snatch back our marriage license for lack of spawn. I've never really understood all this uproar. It's truly baffling. Somehow I get the idea that folks think same-sex marriages are so attractive that their children will be vacuumed right up into one, emerging with good taste and a lively sense of humor, and then where will we be? But it isn't catching. (It's a gift.) In the article, it is explained that opponents of same-sex marriage believe it will "render men and women inter-changeable." Well, *that* clears it up. Because that's a real concern. Right there in Vermont, a young fellow was just fined for shooting a doe illegally. He went to a considerable amount of trouble to drill and fasten antlers to her with lag bolts and epoxy and pass her off as a buck. So you can see people aren't making this stuff up; they see it every day.

Still, it all makes me a little cranky. I'm assuming that all the people who feel this way will eventually wander to the ends of the earth and fall off, and the rest of us will have our nicely spinning planet to ourselves. As to the possums, as far as I'm concerned, they can come back any time. I don't care *how* they're hanging.

Where Does The Dime Go?

My niece Sara, who flits with ease across the planet, from Germany to Tanzania to Washington, D.C., came home to Portland for a few days over Christmas between flits, and then she flitted off to Aspen. It was wonderful seeing her in person, however briefly. Just about as soon as she had left, I thought: dang. I totally forgot to tell her about the turtle lady.

Then I realized: this isn't the nineteenth century. I have lots of ways I can still tell her about the turtle lady. I could write about it longhand with a goose quill and blob it with sealing wax. Or I can send her an email. Then I thought: dang. She isn't going to be at her home for a week and I want to tell her now. Then I thought: dang. She's probably got something the size of a matchbook right in her hip pocket that snags emails out of thin air before they get lost in the series of tubes. She's thirty; she has satellites out there working for her twenty-four hours a day.

Or I could call her. She has a petite phone right there in the other hip pocket and I could waltz right over to the phone I have, stuck in the wall, and call her right up, and there she'd be, and I could tell her about the turtle lady. Trouble is, I hate talking on the phone. There was a year or so in eleventh grade when I spent hours on the phone every night talking to my best friend Janice, but that cured me for life. I saw my first Cellular Mobile Phone when I was on a bicycle tour in the early 90's. They first appeared as disturbing Bricks of Mystery in the back of people's Spandex shorts, but when they pulled them out and punched numbers into them with their big meaty fists, the rest of us were jealous; we were standing in long lines to use the few public phones set up for us in camp. I still didn't want one. But as they became smaller and more ubiquitous, it was easy to see their usefulness. What if, for instance, you were standing in the meat aisle and couldn't decide for yourself whether to go with pork chops or chicken? You could call home and make someone else decide. Or what if you were on your way to Tyler's house and couldn't call him to say you were at 33rd and Broadway about to hang a left through that pack of screaming pedestrians and you'd be there in five minutes? Now you could. What if you were in line at the store and got the urge to call Shaniqua and tell her you were in line at the store? Not a problem.

Still, I haven't bought one. I probably will some day, but I really don't like talking on the phone. And I don't know how to use one. I have to be shown every time. One day at work a guy handed me his phone to talk to someone on the other end, and I kept trying to move the phone from my ear to my mouth to talk, it was so little, even though this didn't appear to be necessary. Finally we signed off, and I didn't know how to hang up, so I folded the little phone up with a snap, and then flew into a prompt panic. Was the person I was talking to still in there? Did I smoosh him? I had quite the little audience by that time, and the expressions ranged from frank amusement to something approaching horror.

I had an Uncle Bill, and the least weird thing about him was that he lived in the rank San Joaquin Hotel for Men in San Francisco. The lobby was redolent of medicine and pee, and he had a small room down the hall with a neatly made cot. I had sought him out, and this inspired him to go visit the rest of his family, all of whom had thought themselves rid of him decades before. He went on a trans-national trek on Greyhound, a tiny, nearly blind, frequently soused man clutching his life's savings in a fat wad of rolled-up bills. It was scary. He spent no more than a half day at any relative's house—North Carolina, Maine, Oregon—before climbing back on the bus. When he asked to use the telephone in our home,

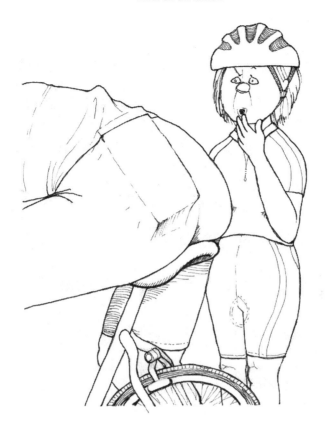

we watched in disbelief as he fumbled with a handful of quarters and dimes, looking for a slot to put them in. I couldn't believe anyone, in 1977, could be that out of it. And now I realize that that's how my friends feel about me.

I don't care. I don't want a cell phone. I want to leave my internet plugged into the wall so I can walk away from it. And although they may already make products that will bring all the world's knowledge to my hip pocket, none of this technology will be available to me until they figure out a way I can retrieve information by sticking a thumb up my butt. Because that's going to be my default stance.

So if anyone sees my niece Sara, tell her there's a lady in Hillsboro who's been able to teach turtles to draw.

Ticketmonster

Last summer we got the word that Bonnie Raitt and Taj Mahal were coming to town on the same ticket. Should we go? Oh, yes. It's $68 apiece! Oh, no.

We held off for a while, to give the rationalization process a chance to crank up. Then we climbed back on line and aimed at a pair of tickets, general admission. The electronic gate was presided over by Ticketmaster. I gave Dave the running score. "Okay, that's $136 for the tickets. Then there's $9 for processing, $14 for a facilities fee, and another $9 for the convenience fee. Times two."

When the air returned to the room, Dave demanded to know what a convenience fee was. It was unclear. So we decided to walk downtown, where there was a ticket office for the venue. It was a seven-mile hike. It was cold, it was raining. We strode up to the box office and asked for two tickets to the BonTaj Tour. The man in the booth totted everything up and asked for an amount of money that was so huge, we made him break it down. "And $18 for the convenience fee," he finished up.

"Convenience fee?" I hollered, stamping the rain out of my boots. "Why not just call it a Corpulence fee? or an Impertinence fee? Or..."

The man regarded me with a bland expression. "It's a corpulence fee," he said.

So I was on full alert when I learned that Ticketmaster is planning to merge with its rival, Live Nation, and pretty much corner the ticket-sales business. So far, the British Department of Justice thinks it's a fine idea, as far as it goes, and that can be a long way. Because, honey? It won't stop there.

Welcome to MasterNation, where we offer all the tools you need to service yourself in the privacy of your own home. All right! Let's get started. We've put you down for two tickets to the upcoming Tom Waits-Yo Yo Ma concert, and...

Wait a minute. I didn't order any—whoa! Did you say Tom Waits and Yo Yo Ma are coming to town?

Eventually. Yo Yo Ma plays with everybody.

Well I have to admit that sounds wonderful. Where do I click to pay?

Oh you've already paid. Thanks to our newest partnerships with AccuVac and Chase Manhattan, we've been siphoning money out of your checking account in modest, regular increments, building you a sound down-payment structure for the future. You won't even notice it, did you? And with our complimentary rate-comparison feature, thanks to last week's merger with Progressive Insurance, you can shop for the best loan rates to make up the difference.

That is convenient. But I've never given you the password to my accounts.

Sure you have. We just employed our simple, patented algorithm using the information you supplied to the Facebook app during "What's your pirate name" week.

Arrrr.

And we'll be sending you your tickets via the Postal Service, as you always prefer. There will be an additional shipping charge of $10.00. The Post Office doesn't charge that much to mail two tickets.

That includes the Postal Service Destruction Fee. We'd rather you used our preferred partner, UPS. You'll get your tickets inside of a week, and you can re-use the box. Don't fret—your account is plumping up nicely. You've already got enough in there to cover the Walter-Tops Tour, even with the you're-not-paying-attention surcharge.

"I've never heard of the Walter-Tops."

You will. You'll like them.

"How in the world can you know that?"

We have a new association with one of the finest search engines on the planet.

"Yahoo. But how can you be sure who I'm going to want to see?"

That's not a problem, Clickenheimer. Go ahead and answer the door, I'll wait.

The doorbell rang.

It was a hot lonely Russian blonde. She wished meeting for ride my love pony.

Chapter 5

Fun With Dave

~

Blood, Simple
Next, A Moose Head
The Poot
Dispatch From The Belfry
Hard Workers Never Pump Their Own
A Bunny Tale
The Ants Are Back
Vampires Among Us
The Whiz Kid
I Incyst

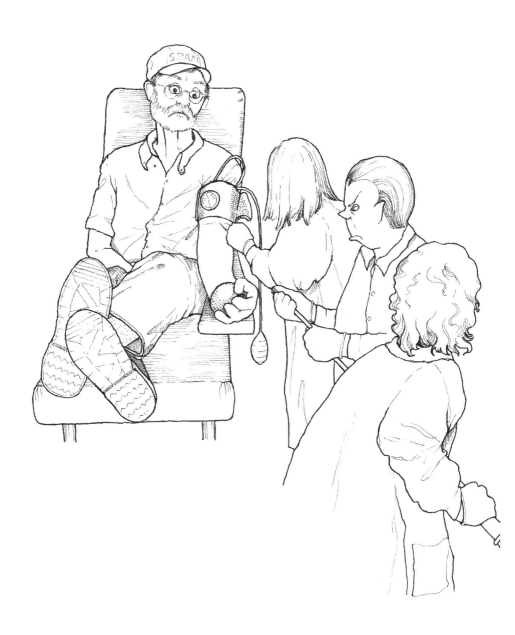

Blood, Simple

Since we've retired, we've looked for excuses to take walks. For instance, if I suddenly need a tiny plastic mountain goat, and never mind why, then we walk six miles to the tiny plastic mountain goat store downtown and buy one. So when I made an appointment to give blood at Red Cross, which is only three miles away, I invited Dave along. He hesitated. "You're supposed to drink extra fluids afterwards," I wheedled. "There's a brewpub a few blocks from the Red Cross that pours $2.50 pints on Tuesdays." Sold!

I've been giving blood for almost forty years, so I have an impressive tally of pints shed. The people at the blood donor center invariably express their gratitude and make it seem as though I've done a really stellar thing. I haven't. If someone, right now, told you she'd do something to you that stung for a nanosecond in exchange for a nap on a lounge chair and a faceful of donuts, would you go for it? Me too.

But Dave has always refused to go. Needles give him the willies. "Can't they take it with a knife?" he always says. He doesn't have many vulnerabilities, but if you Tivo the scene in that movie when Nick Nolte is getting a huge needle in the knee, you can get a whole lot of mileage out of it.

Dave says he did try to give blood once as a teenager but it was a dreadful experience, right up to the point where everything went black. He has a long way to fall, and witnesses reported the moaning sound triggered the Doppler effect. For a few days they just swept around him. Empires rose and fell.

But the man do love to walk. We took off for the Red Cross. I re-assured him that they never miss my vein, even though it's small and hard to see, whereas his veins jut and jump like cobras. Still, I looked around for one of the exceptional blood-drawers for him. You want a phlebotomist who shows a lot of confidence. Unfortunately, that doesn't weed out the sadists. Dave drew the fellow with the wild grey mullet and the Jack Nicholson leer, and that fellow had at him for several minutes, reducing his left arm to pulp, until the trainer came up and offered to take a stab at it.

The trainer, opting for the next arm over, went for a quick and graceful poke, then another, then another ten or twelve, and finally, through sheer force of will, he drilled in and mined some sort of deep aquifer and the well sprang forth. Dave's expression was rigid and staring. A young man nearby fainted dead away. I figured that was Dave's last blood donation.

Nevertheless, eight weeks later, Dave again accompanied me to the Red Cross, theorizing it couldn't be worse, and it wasn't. It was exactly the same. Bruises in both arms bloomed like oil slicks on the sea, and days later folks were still edging away from him in the grocery line. I wouldn't have blamed him for calling it quits. But last week he accompanied me yet again. This time he had gone for the Needle-phobe's Perfecta. He had spent that very morning at Kaiser getting a cortisone shot in his frozen shoulder. "Was it a huge needle?" I queried. Dave shuddered. "The guy who pushed the plunger was in the next room," he said. At the donor center, we got ourselves settled into the lounge chairs. Dave was approached by a pony-tailed young woman who might have passed for thirteen. She sized him up, flicked her needle and slid it home, and Dave's blood leapt up and shot out into the bag in four and a half minutes.

Meanwhile, my blood was drooling out, spiraling down the tube with all the gusto of a seven-year-old on his way to bed. A team of phlebotomists stood around with frowns and thumped my arm and jiggled my needle and made fretting noises. Fifteen minutes later, my life force was still dribbling into the bag in a manner usually described as "ebbing away."

Both Dave and I have fine blood—A+, in fact, although Dave points out that I got an F in sex—and I hope our respective pints will have some salutary effect on somebody, somewhere. Although whoever gets mine might have to wait.

Next, A Moose Head

Electronic devices have topped the list of preferred gifts for normal American males for years now, and for years Dave has asked for an elephant's-foot wastebasket for Christmas. You can draw any conclusion from that that you wish, including that Dave is an antique or possibly deceased British gentleman from the Raj era given to monocles, pipe-smoking and imperialism. Or, he is not normal. As you prefer. It's all the same to me.

But a while back I decided the only way to get him to quit asking for such a revolting item would be to make him one. First step is to look it up online, and sure enough, there is such a thing as a wastebasket made of a sawed-off elephant's foot, and there is no effort made to pretty it up. Anyone who has one of these objects in his possession is seriously depraved, and no mistake. I know there is a tendency towards hyperbole these days, days in which failing to strap a bike helmet on your child constitutes abuse, and meat is murder, but I will state here unequivocally that owning an elephant's-foot wastebasket is way worse than eating a hamburger.

One night I concocted a plan involving ceramic elephant toenails and batting and fabric and flour paste and a lot of criss-crossing with dental floss to simulate wrinkles, with the intention of removing the floss once the fabric is dry. It beats staying awake worrying about your finances, although it's just as effective from an insomnia point of view. Once I got the toenails back from the kiln, it was going to have to be a quick operation so as to achieve full wrinkle while the foot was still wet. You never know how these things are going to work out until you try: as the old saying goes, nothing ventured, nothing fancy to toss your toilet-paper tube in. Well, it didn't work so well. I couldn't keep the fabric straight, and it tended to wrinkle up on its own, so I changed gears and went with that, only it took more and more fabric, until finally I had about forty bucks invested in cotton elephant skin. If I'd had to take down a real elephant, though, I'm sure it would have cost a lot more, even if I sold off the other three wastebaskets.

Dave ain't right, but he ain't bad, either, and he probably envisioned the wastebasket as the perfect accessory for his beloved bathroom, which he designed himself with wainscoting and dentil molding and nickel-plated faucets and a marble floor and an art collection. He spends an awful lot of time in there and it pleases him to have fancy surroundings, even if all he's doing is the same thing England did to India.

The Poot

I should probably explain about Pootie. Pootie, who is currently in charge of our house, arrived here stowed away in a ribboned box on Christmas day, 1988. Although he is frequently mistaken for a bear, which doesn't bother him, or a bunny, which does, he is a dog. Technically, a stuffed dog. But if his head is packed with lint, it only means he's gotten the jump on the rest of us.

Pootie is a dog given to firm opinions and well-defined preferences, and from the early days it was clear that many of them aligned closely with Dave's. For instance, he enjoys making a public spectacle of himself, he loves chocolate, and he adores basketball. Dave would consult with Pootie, listen carefully, and say, "Pootie wants to know"—the Poot would nod vigorously—"Pootie wants to know if there are any chocolate chip cookies left." Or, "Pootie wants to know if there's any reason we couldn't turn on the Lakers game." That was actually the only deviation, however slight, that Pootie took from the Dave canon. Although both man and dog were fervent basketball fans, Dave rooted for the Portland Trailblazers and Pootie was a die-hard for the Los Angeles Lakers. He even began to bald a bit on top, revealing a neat row of stitching, just like his hero, Kareem Abdul-Jabbar. We snuck Pootie into the Blazer games whenever we attended, always eluding the security at the gate, to the Poot's immense satisfaction. He always wore his own Lakers sweats, just to be provocative, and someone would always cheerfully offer to rip his head off.

Pootie gets to go everywhere with us, including seven consecutive trips on the Cycle Oregon bicycle tour, when he rode up front on the

handlebars on his own personal Barkalounger sporting helmet and official t-shirt, courting fame and admiration. ("Oh, look at the cute bear! Oh, look at the little t-shirt! Oh, look at that helmet!" some admiring female would say; then, to me, "you don't have any kids, do you?")

Still, although Pootie is our constant companion, I was actually moved when Dave took him to watch the All-Star game. We were at our cabin, a space sanctified by the absence of television, on a snowy February weekend, when Dave asked if I wanted to pop into the nearest tavern to watch the basketball game. I didn't. I had a book. So Dave took off for a few hours, tucking Pootie into his jacket, and inviting him to recline against the napkin dispenser to observe the goings-on. While he was gone I thought of what a special fellow Dave is. Many, if not all, men would be loath to bring a (technically) stuffed dog into a tavern for the purposes of watching a sports game on TV, but it hadn't even occurred to Dave to leave Pootie behind. More I thought of it, the more I was filled with love for Dave and his compassion for the little fuzzy people in life. I told him so when they came back. "You know, most guys wouldn't have taken someone like Pootie to a bar," I said, with a catch in my throat. Dave shrugged it off. It was nothing.

"Pootie," he said significantly, "is a babe magnet."

Dispatch From The Belfry

Night before last, I felt something crawling on my back and discovered a largish ant in bed with me. He seemed to be working solo, but I couldn't imagine what an ant was doing there, and even after I took care of the offender, I felt kind of itchy all night. *What next?* I thought. Rhetorically, I thought.

Then last night, Dave mentioned that it sounded like our cat Tater was having one of her standard epizootics in our bedroom. If this had occurred during the reign of our previous cat Larry, we would have concluded she was on High Moth Alert. But with Tater, it was more likely to be a random firing of her rambunction gene. I headed upstairs, walked into the bedroom and flipped on the light.

Bat. Bat bat bat. Giant bat doing laps in the airspace. Now, I like bats. In context. The context being outdoors. I love to watch them swing through the air like a celebration of twilight. I once saw one in the zoo hanging upside down and—well. Entertaining himself. It was something.

With a bat *in my bedroom*, however, I lost all decorum. I went all 1950s-sitcom-wife over the thing. I hit the carpet like (as I later discovered) guano, and yelled the same thing over and over again (a major religious figure plus a salty adjective). Bats have acute hearing and possibly demure sensibilities as well, and this couldn't have been pleasant for it. I'm not proud of my reaction, and it's hard to justify it when you see the photograph I took of our wayward mammal. She's all folded up just like a little wallet; but airborne, I am here to tell you, she has the wingspan and demeanor of a pterodactyl. Dave came to the rescue and tried to encourage her out the window, but she was not persuaded. Instead she flew into the closet and hung herself up somewhere on his clothing (gabardine, rayon, cotton, bat, flannel), making extraordinary little scolding noises, rattling like a string of beads. Among the things Dave did that I was incapable of doing at that point was to lean into his shirts and blow on them ("I didn't want to hurt the bat").

Ultimately, Dave managed to coax the bat into flapping around the room again and he nabbed her with a short-handled fishing net, stepping nimbly around my prostrate form. He mused later that it would have made more sense to open all the windows, turn out all the lights and shut the door, and the bat would have found her own way out. And she probably would have, too, but if I hadn't seen her exit, I would have never gone to bed or changed my clothes again.

It's entertaining, being in a room with a bat and a black cat, but it's not restful. I had to eat a whole bowl of eyeballs just to settle down.

Hard Workers Never Pump Their Own

I couldn't tell you how old I was the day it happened; I only know that I still had a good supporting cast of hormones, but my youthful muscle tone was already looking for a new gig. I was riding my bicycle home from work, and someone was directly behind me in the bike lane for several miles, keeping pace but not passing. When I sheared off to the right, he called out, in tones that still reverberate through the winds of time, "You have a great butt!"—a little item I endeavored to work into my conversations several times over the next few weeks, until finally, in a bid for closure, someone said, "well, you can't put a price tag on that." Actually, I can. I'd have put it at a good buck-forty-five anyway, and that was before I realized how rare it was. Now, what with demand regularly exceeding supply, and inflation, personal and otherwise, I'd go quite a bit more. There are days I'd empty my wallet for it.

There's got to be a whole untapped market out there. I can't be the only person who would be willing to fork over cold cash to someone who knows just how to make other people feel really good, maybe a little tingly. Why, it could be the basis for a whole profession.

Dave contends it's his job to say things like the fellow on the bicycle did, although he didn't get all prickly about it. He can't. He's got a girlfriend at the gas station. He used to swing by the Union 76 on his way home from work because it was the closest. Dave worked very, very hard in his job. He's been known to use a ninety-pound jackhammer over his head for twelve hours in a boiler at 110 degrees. He'd run through a pair of overalls and ten pairs of

gloves in a week. He'd come home gashed and sooty. Sometimes he'd just burst into flame. Then he'd cook my dinner and maybe kiss my paper cuts.

The gas station is owned and operated by a Vietnamese family, and the matriarch of the crew is something special. Even I can see that. She's not a young thing; certainly no younger than we are. She has a beautiful daughter who looks very much like her, but it is the older woman who really knows how to handle the hose.

She would lean into the window, tip her head up and smile. *Are those flower petals in the air?* And ask what Dave wanted today. *Is that music I hear?* And one day, as Dave was handing over his cash, she stopped and turned his hand over and over, stroking the calloused rind on the palm side and tracing his knuckles with a delicate finger, and breathed, "Ho-aaah. You work haa-aaahd for a living." And removed the cash, and turned her face up to his, all sweetness and cherry blossoms. Eventually Dave got the truck into gear and remembered the way home.

She's not there every time, but as has been demonstrated with rats and pellets, random reward really pulls the lasso tight. What kind of price tag can you hang on that? The Union 76 charges twenty cents more than anyone else for gas, and Dave's been going there for ten years now.

A Bunny Tale

Sometimes we don't know our own true nature until circumstance shines a light on us and reveals who we really are. A callow youth dives into turbulent waves to save a child. A skipper gives himself up to pirates to save his crew. A wealthy and proud evangelist blubbers like a baby when he's caught with a hooker. What struck me most, when the light of circumstance shone on me, was how very bright it was.

I have the honor of living with a 62-year-old man who believes in nothing regular at all—not God, not the invisible hand of the marketplace, not even Santa Claus—nothing except the Easter Bunny. And about him he is fervent. The Easter Bunny has come through for Dave every year of his entire life, and if he couldn't count on the Buns, his entire belief structure would wither like a retirement plan. But the world spins on, the daphne blooms anew, and the house is pocked with hidden chocolate every spring. He and his friend Pootie gambol about like spring lambs and fill up a large basket.

I am not the Easter Bunny. I am not delusional. No, I am but an assistant and concierge to E.B., responsible merely for opening the door after it has been determined that Dave is deep in slumber. The Bunny is admitted and allowed to go about his business. Only, Dave is pretty tall, and a lot of the best hiding places are hard for the bunny to reach, so I started helping. And the Bunny has a mighty packed schedule, so I started to help a little more. And, what with one thing and another, and the worldwide proliferation of Christians and all, now it's kind of down to the Bunny letting me know where he does his shopping, and calling it a day. Anyway, we're tight.

One Easter morning, early, 2am, in 2001, I crept out of bed to let the Easter Bunny in, and hung around as usual to help. I don't wear jammies to bed and didn't see any particular reason to put any on; it was a warm night, and all the lights were off in the house. I was nearly through hiding the stash when I decided to stack some truffles up high, on top of the window frame. So I planted both feet a comfortable distance apart on the back of the sofa, reached way up with my left hand to hold onto the window frame, and way up with my right to position the truffles. That left all my sticky-outy bits pressed against the window glass. And that would be the moment a car began to approach down the street, but since the headlights were aligned with the street rather than in my direction, it did not appear to be a problem. Unless the car suddenly swung towards the curb in front of the house next door, which is just what it did, pinning me with a halogen spotlight in an essentially—let's just say it—crucified pose. Our brand-new, perfectly adorable young male neighbors were home from the tavern. Alleluia!

I do not know if the perfectly adorable young men were looking up at the window they were illuminating, twenty feet away. But if they were, I am proud to say they saw me as I truly am. The Deputy to the Easter Bunny.

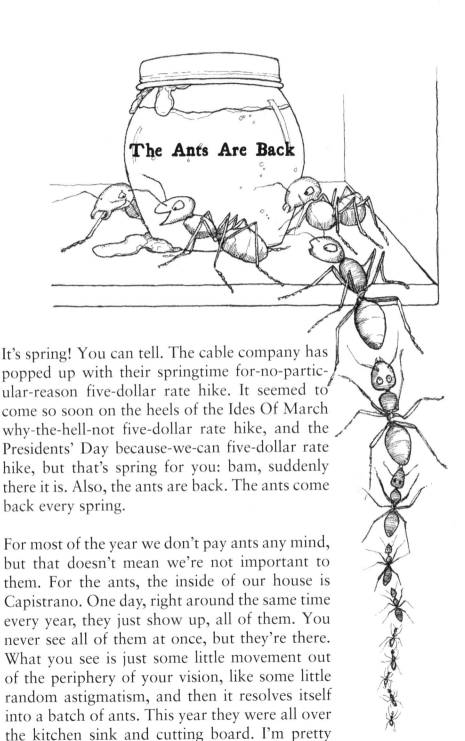

The Ants Are Back

It's spring! You can tell. The cable company has popped up with their springtime for-no-partic-ular-reason five-dollar rate hike. It seemed to come so soon on the heels of the Ides Of March why-the-hell-not five-dollar rate hike, and the Presidents' Day because-we-can five-dollar rate hike, but that's spring for you: bam, suddenly there it is. Also, the ants are back. The ants come back every spring.

For most of the year we don't pay ants any mind, but that doesn't mean we're not important to them. For the ants, the inside of our house is Capistrano. One day, right around the same time every year, they just show up, all of them. You never see all of them at once, but they're there. What you see is just some little movement out of the periphery of your vision, like some little random astigmatism, and then it resolves itself into a batch of ants. This year they were all over the kitchen sink and cutting board. I'm pretty low-tech about ants. I mash-and-wipe with a hot sponge, repeating as necessary. I try to get to them before Dave does, because he loses his mind around insects. It's a good thing we live in Oregon, where we are able to fling open our windows all summer without putting in screens. If he lived in Africa, or Florida, or really almost anywhere else in the country, he'd flat perish from the willies.

If Dave sees the ants first, he will apply some sort of spray insecticide to the thickness of a paste all over. The ants will drown long before they have an opportunity to succumb to malathion poisoning. I hate this, but I've learned to accept that he cannot help himself. Since, every spring, he also gets a notion to clean all the windows in the house inside and out, I've learned to overlook some of his other issues.

The thing is, I may be onto the ants before he is, but I never seem to get the big picture right away. I'll be mashing and wiping ants in about the same location for two, three days, and then on the fourth day I'll notice that they seem to be coming from a little distance away, and I'll follow them backwards with the sponge, and eventually I'll look up and there will be a major vertical column of ants going up the wall, enough to make the walls look slimmer. The ant stripe is visible from the next room if you happen to be looking at the right spot, so it's hard to imagine how I had missed them before. It's as though you see something shiny, and you think, hmmm: that almost looks a little bit like a claw, only way larger, and then you look up and discover you're crouching at the foot of a tyrannosaur. The ants have obviously been there all along, and you can trace them to a little bloop of raspberry jam on the second shelf of the cabinet. You can tidy that up and wipe down the ants and in any case they'd have been gone in another week, but it's still a heck of an operation they're running. No doubt one scout ant located the stash and alerted the whole platoon.

It's impressive. You can't even get ten humans in a sushi bar to figure out how to split the check.

Vampires Among Us

The first mosquito was annoying. It wasn't until I slapped the second, a minute or two later, that I was flooded with panic. It hit me like that white flash of shock you get when you've only popped into the store for some cigarettes and maybe one video poker game and suddenly a few hours later you remember you've left the kids in the car with the windows rolled up and a case of Ho Hos and a little bottle of something to help you get some sleep. Pure dread.

I ran around the place looking for my strong, lean, brave man but when I found him it was too late. He was already slumped over, whimpering, drained, anemic, and a little pudgy. The pudge was due to a uniform layer of fused welts swelling his body a half inch in every direction. "I'm gonna die," he said.

He doesn't scare easily. This is the guy who maintained for years that "anybody can quit smoking. It takes a man to face lung cancer."

Mosquitoes adore Dave. They plan their holidays around him. When they're done with him they all go off and lie down, patting their bellies and burping and maybe watching a little football. For years we have employed him at barbecues to stand a little off to the side and draw mosquitoes. They'd be ecstatic. We'd hear them yelling "Wheeeeeeeeeeeeeeeeeeeeee-ooooooooooo!" with the Doppler effect kicking in as they zoomed overhead. If we brought him enough hot dogs he'd stand over there all afternoon and smack himself like a masochist with Tourette's.

One day, in Maine, my sister and Dave and I walked through a mosquito-drenched forest to get to the beach. We expected the beach to be windy enough to repel mosquitoes and it was, except not *these* mosquitoes. Dave bailed out in fear when he got to the water and discovered they were still there. He ran a mile back to the car, shut himself and a few hundred mosquitoes inside and maniacally slapped the living crap out of every surface in it. Anyone happening upon the scene would have been concerned enough to call the authorities, after pulling back a few miles.

We're not supposed to have mosquitoes in Portland. Screen porches are unknown. We only keep screens on a couple of windows to keep the cat in. Even Dave gets no more than a bite a night at worst, from the single mosquito in a mile radius. But suddenly this year we have mosquitoes, and their arrival coincided with the temperatures rising to near a thousand degrees, and at night we left a couple windows open a crack, leaving all the lights off. Dave woke up with a mosquito biting his lip, which swelled tremendously. He looked like Angelina Jolie with a beard, which is surprisingly attractive. "What more can I do?" he wailed, and other than trying it again the next night with his pants off, I couldn't think of a thing.

The reason we have mosquitoes this year is the record-breaking rains we had in May and June, brought to us by the same folks that brought unseasonal snow, monster hurricanes and successive hundred-year floods. Mainly people like James "Global Warming Is A Hoax" Inhofe, who also doesn't think much of universal health care. If Dave ever gets out of the ICU, that's who I'm sending the bill to.

The Whiz Kid

Citizens of Toronto are on the alert for a band of pickpockets who distract their victims by strafing them with fecal matter. The perpetrators work in concert, one flinging poo, one pointing out the flung poo, and one executing the robbery, and presumably all share the profits, although I should think that the one in charge of collecting ammunition might rate a bonus. Underpaid employees of Forensics have confirmed the fecal matter to be human. Which brings two observations to mind. One: Evolution is not all it's cracked up to be. Two: at least they're not using the fake stuff.

There is a disturbing trend towards the use of phony bodily humors and something really should be done before it gets out of hand. Faux poo and blood are still mostly used in the novelty industry, and the mock mucus market is still in its infancy, being mostly confined to a single storefront in Pittsburgh. (Its product, "I-Can't-Believe-It's-Not-Booger," has remained stuck on the shelves, and the proprietor blames slow sales on the economy. He rigorously denies that his product is illegal. "That blows," he told reporters recently. "It's not," he is believed to have added.)

The most egregious use of fake humors is the trade in false bile, truckloads of which are off-loaded to the Republican National Committee daily, which resolutely defends its use. "We have way too much legislation to thwart to be limited to authentic indignation," a spokesman said.

But the fake fluid most alarming in its implications, for my money, is the thriving market in false urine. Perhaps I take this a bit too

personally, but Dave's and my entire lifestyle is built on a founda-
tion of genuine American pee.

Dave recently retired from a career as a refractory hod carrier,
a position which frequently required him to work long shifts in
boilers so hot that the wheelbarrow tire would explode and the
plank it was running on would catch fire. Workers were sealed
up in these areas and given a gallon of water an hour and let out
only after their juices ran clear when they were poked with a fork.
It's not a job for everybody, but union wages did attract a small
number of men to sign up. Then, in the eighties, drug screen-
ing tests became routine. Of the tiny subset of humans willing
to do Dave's kind of work, an astonishing number at any given
time were lacking their driver's licenses or their freedom; and although many could still pass urine, far fewer could pass a urine
test. Dave might have been among these except for his foresight in
developing a broad and diversified portfolio of vices, so it was a
simple matter of re-balancing these and presto—full employment
for Dave. "Crap," the foreman would say, "we'll be needing a
dozen drug-free guys for the Hoffman job," and our phone would
ring, and Dave would join a small group of other men who were
probably sleeping it off when they got the call.

Ultimately, it was not his stellar work ethic, his stamina, his
strength, or his willingness to endure pain that got him these jobs,
although all of those became important in his marriage. It was his
pee. Dave's pee was golden.

But now, it turns out, workers have been cheating the tests with false
urine for years. Some have employed the urine of other animals,
resulting in a workforce that tests negative for marijuana but positive for hoof-and-mouth. But most have purchased, legally, vials of
synthetic urine. Sometimes these can be detected by underpaid lab
employees by smell alone, but not always. It's scandalous. It's
changed the whole game.

But for thirty years, Bromley Masonry, C. H. Murphy Refractory and I all had something in common. Dave was our number-one guy.

I Incyst

My husband Dave and I just came back from the hospital, where he underwent a surgical procedure to evict a cyst from personal territory. The cyst was benign but uncomfortable. For Dave, that is; the cyst itself was probably snug as a bug. Everything seems to be okay so far. The entire admitting process was reassuring. A series of folks in scrubs came in to ask questions, one after the other, pretty much the same questions, all designed to make sure they had the right person on the gurney and were all planning to do the same thing in the same location. When you're operating in highly personal territory, you want everyone on the same page. I've just read where this sort of redundancy actually does reduce the number of errors. So everyone who came in wanted Dave to tell them who he was, and they all got the same answer every time, even after they'd slipped the joy juice in his I.V. and he might have been inclined to tell them he was Princess Margaret. And they asked him the same question I also get with every visit: is there anyone at home you're afraid of? "Absolutely," Dave said solemnly, and the nurses glanced at me and burst out laughing. [Note to self: develop an edge.] Anyway, all personnel were professional and cheerful and calm, and there would have been no reason to feel anything but confidence except that Dave had already been in for this precise procedure four years ago.

After that one, there was plenty of discomfort and outright pain and it went on for weeks and weeks, until finally—not wanting to seem like a complainer—Dave called up his surgeon with a few questions. The surgeon was dismissive. He explained that he'd done *this* to *that* and so of course there was going to be some pain.

Now Dave is not a whiny man, and doesn't care to have it implied that he is, and he does has a high tolerance for pain. I mean, he's not going to sit through a Michael Bolton concert or anything, but still. So he carried on best he could for a few months and when there was still no relief, he insisted on an ultrasound to check things out.

The ultrasound technician said everything looked just fine. "Except for this cyst over here," he added, "but it's benign." "Benign" is all well and good, but "begone" was more what we were going for. It was as if the surgeon had plunged down to the murky depths, pried open an oyster, snapped it shut again, and come back up with the bends and the willies, and when asked where the pearl was, said: "Pearl?" It all seems so pointless. It's a lot of trouble for nothing. It's going to Paris for a Big Mac.

So this time we arrived wary and lawyered-up. Not really; we're not litigious sorts, but between the last surgery and this surgery, our nephew had passed the bar, and that should count for something. He mostly represents condo owners who are suing construction companies for shoddy workmanship, which is not particularly germane to this case. But still, going with him seems like a better bet than threatening someone with our niece, the Peace Corps worker.

The surgeon came out to the waiting room right after this last procedure to tell me that everything went well. That's what he told me four years ago, too. He sent us home with a bunch of bandages and a bucket of Oxycodone, but I should have asked for the pearl, too. The nurse in Recovery gave us instructions and supplies, and he also told me that I should be giving Dave foot-rubs, even though that's nowhere near the surgery site. Dave's home now, resting up, but our cat, Tater, with her unerring instinct for the exact square foot in the house she is least welcome, is sizing up his lap, tail twitching. If anyone needs me, I'll be a half mile down the street.

Chapter 6

The Present Murr

A Cure For Cancer
A Hell Of A Potter
Late-Breaking Mews
Under Cover In West Virginia
Die Hard, With A Backpack
Merriweather
The Numbers Racket
Pinned Down
Music Of The Spheres
Round Feet

A Cure For Cancer

When I was much younger, I could get really good and sick and not read a thing into it. That's all changed. For instance, a couple months ago I developed a little strain in my front ribcage. Merely by spending my waking hours thinking about it, I got the little strain to show up on the back of the ribcage too. I could only feel it when I inhaled deeply and pressed into it with a fork. Naturally, I concluded it was cancer. Let other people ignore symptoms until it's too late; I'm going to be proactive.

I got a chest x-ray (normal, but what do they know?) and made an appointment with a doctor, and in the meantime I went to my massage therapist, Maria. She's scary strong, but she uses her powers for good. Still, I almost didn't mention the whole ribcage thing, because I was pretty sure it was cancer, and not part of her terrain. She listened, and peered at my midsection for a moment, and then rolled up her sleeves and told me she'd fix it. She wasn't even wearing sleeves. That's how strong she is.

I've been to a number of massage therapists over the years, and there are as many styles and methods as there are practitioners. It always feels good, but some of them aren't really giving themselves what I'd call a workout. Some of them just tap on you as though their fingertips were petals, or blessings. Some of them just massage your aura. Some of them even leave the room, probably for a cigarette, after laying warm rocks on you, which is perfectly pleasant if you don't think of it as the beginning of being buried alive.

But Maria is determined to set you straight, or make you swear up and down that she did. First she oils up. (It smells great, but I'm pretty sure it's bear grease; I believe I saw the unfortunate grease donors stacked up outside in the alley after she strangles them. Could be cardboard boxes, but I think it's bears.) Then she starts moving parts of you around to see how far they'll go before they snap off. Basically it's the same thing you do to the chicken to see if it's done. She waggles your leg around counterclockwise: first to nine o'clock, then to six, and by the time she's gotten to three o'clock, you've briefly glimpsed parts of yourself you'd only heard described by others.

As far as I can tell, Maria's plan is to remove your muscle fibers, one by one, from their moorings, straighten out your skeleton, and then re-attach the muscles when everything is all plumb and square. She pulls your musculature away from the bones and hangs it up somewhere nearby so it doesn't wrinkle. I would have thought the little muscles along the ribcage would be tough to spring loose, but she didn't have a problem with it; just got a grip on the spleen, wedged her knee on the liver and pulled upward on the sternum. Then she tucked the unattached muscle fibers under the gallbladder and did a half-hitch with an intestine loop to get them out of the way until she was ready to stick them back on again.

From there, straightening out the skeleton was a breeze. She only needed to whack at about a third of it, and threaten the rest, which fell into line out of sheer terror.

It's been a week. My cancer is gone. I swear it, up and down.

A Hell Of A Potter

When I met my friend Peg thirty years ago, she was a young hippie potter. As people will, she cycled through a number of grown-up gigs after that, like real estate, until now. Now she's an old hippie potter. Specifically, she makes Raku, an ancient tradition in which the mystery of clay is wedded to the romance of self-immolation. At least that's how I see it.

It's a solitary art, but there are a few odd steps in the making of Raku that go a lot easier if there's a helper. I volunteered to help, because I'm five minutes away and am never doing anything important. She assured me the whole operation would take about five or ten minutes and would not be a big deal; just a matter of putting garbage can lids on garbage cans and tossing a few wet towels around, and I've done both of those things before. In fact, I like to think I'm right at the head of the pack for wet-towel-tossing. The main point was to be there at the moment one is needed. I arrived full of confidence in my abilities, because if there's one thing I can do well, it's show up.

So I get there, and it turns out there's an outfit. There's a bright silver asbestos apron, there are welder's gloves, there's a *freakin'* gas mask, and it occurs to me, as Peg points out the nearby garden hose "in case things get out of hand," that there's more to this operation than just showing up. But time was of the essence, and there was no time for chit-chat. Peg and I lifted the top off the kiln and set it aside, and Peg grabbed some enormous tongs and pulled out her ceramic pieces, placing them one by one into an array of garbage cans filled with shredded paper, and that's when all hell broke loose.

Literally. Fire, brimstone, smoke, acrid odor and the screams of the wretched. The screams were coming from me, I'm told, and I can't discount that as a possibility. I get jumpy. This is why I don't believe in heaven and hell. It's just one more scenario in which I've got a feeling I won't come out well, so I'd rather abstain. On the other hand, if I've missed my guess about this, helping Peg with the Raku is probably going to be good conditioning for me, ultimately.

Still, I'm not that into fire. I grew up outside of Washington, D.C., and I've sought out cool temperatures ever since. As a kid, I didn't give much thought to my future livelihood, but I knew I didn't want to do anything where I was likely to be shot at, or set aflame. Postal work really came pretty close to meeting all my requirements. Oh, sure, there was that time Herbie's Jeep blew up and he ran around in circles screaming "CALL NINE-ELEVEN! CALL NINE-ELEVEN!" and everything went to ashes while people looked for the "eleven" button on their phones. But that's just Herbie, and really, you take enough letter carriers and turn them loose for enough years, one of them is going to set himself on fire. That's just the way it is. As for the business of not getting shot at, the trick is to be a little scarier than the person who might want to shoot you, and with the postal uniform and a slightly unhinged demeanor, you're halfway there.

So here I was, tasked with the job of putting the lids on the garbage cans, which were roaring fire up to the skies, and tossing the wet towels over them, and whereas I do not believe I did such a good job, I'm pretty sure I'll be better next time. I'll show a little more confidence, and maybe, per Peg's excellent suggestion, I won't fling the lids towards the cans like Frisbees and hope for a good seal. "This is why not many people do Raku," Peg kindly explained in a nasal bleat through the gas mask.

But here's why people do. You get this gorgeous stuff, the more wonderful because there's no way to predict what is going to come out of those cans. Postal work is more placid, but the best you can do is finish up on a given day and then have it all to do over again the next morning. So it's like doing the dishes.

And by the time I've done this Raku business a few more times, I'll have gotten a little more accustomed to the weather in hell. When the time comes, I'll be better able to cope. As long as it's not humid.

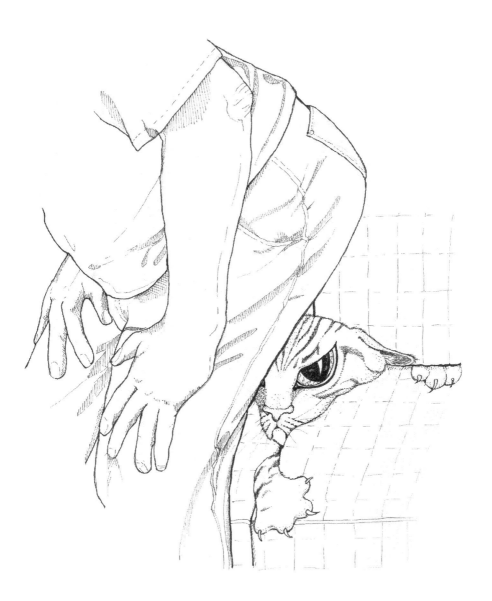

Late-Breaking Mews

I may be the slowest scooper on the parade route, but I would really like to think that if there was a strange cat holed up inside my sofa, I'd be able to figure it out. I'd like to think that if my sofa were mewing, and if I had just purchased the sofa used, and if the mewing began on the day I brought the sofa home, I'd be able to connect some dots. If I were not able to put it all together, I doubt that my first reaction, upon sitting down on the sofa and feeling something move beneath me, would be to pick up the sofa and look. Not unless I could do it from up on the ceiling fan.

A Miss Vickie Mendenhall, of Spokane, however, lived with a yowling davenport for quite a few days before her boyfriend discovered the cat by sitting on it. Perhaps they were distracted. Perhaps they were inattentive by nature. Perhaps the TV was too loud. "It sounds like there's a zebra in the garage," Miss Mendenhall might say. "That Simon Cowell is a tool," the boyfriend would respond, and that would be all there was to that, until someone had to back out the Cherokee.

In reality, though, I might not have been any quicker on the uptake. A lot of times when I hear something, it's just safer all around to assume that no one else can hear it. Recently I began to notice that there was a mild little *eep!* sound every so often when I was sitting at the computer. Dave heard it too, although even we don't consider that a lock on reality. It seemed quite random and was so quiet, like a distant mouse at a surprise party, that we were never able to triangulate it. Out of nowhere would come another *eep!* and we'd both point in different directions, unable to agree on a source. I eventually discovered that it came hourly, at nineteen minutes after. Then I heard it while I was in a whole other room. I suspected my watch itself, and quarantined it upstairs, to no avail. *Eep!* No matter where we were, at nineteen after the hour we heard a little *eep!* coming from somewhere nearby.

When it *eeped* shortly before people were coming for dinner, I got the brilliant idea of setting an alarm for 59 minutes and enlisting the whole crew to listen up. I forgot to tell them about it, though, and when the buzzer sounded, I suddenly jumped up and screamed at everybody. "Mikey! Stand by the basement door! Susan! Over here by the oven! Andrea! Next to the computer! Go, go, *go*! Be very quiet and *listen!*" They all ran to their places, one wondering if he should pick up a weapon, one wondering if she should summon a medical professional. And we found it. Everyone was pointing in the same direction, like it was the grassy knoll. The oven was *eeping*. We have no idea why.

So now it's just another little reminder of the passage of time, and puts me in mind a bit of those moments of existential dread you sometimes get in the middle of the night. Those were a lot scarier when I was younger; it would feel like a pellet of ice hitting my heart, when suddenly, out of nowhere, I would recognize that my own death, far from being hypothetical, was an actual event in my own actual future. It was terrifying. Those moments have come up periodically throughout my life (*eep!*) but over the years I've paid less attention to them. Oh crap, I'm going to die some day, alert the press; boo hoo; now, don't forget to throw some compost on the strawberry patch.

I'm not liable to do anything about the oven, either.

Under Cover In West Virginia

This is your trusty reporter checking in from the New River Birding And Nature Festival, where I have been embedded for a week into a platoon of birders. I am in full birder camo with binoculars and zip-off pants and have undergone training in birder posture, mouth agape and head cranked back in a position known to cause strokes in elderly people. There are plenty of birds who muck about on the ground but we seem to be focusing on warblers in the treetops. Sustained warbler-watching causes a painful condition known as "warbler neck." (The development of streaky chin feathers is a whole different condition.) This can be alleviated with the purchase of a strap-on neck rest, which has the side benefit of maximizing dorkiness, by which solitary birders can recognize each other and possibly pair off.

In groups, birders tend to bunch up and point skyward, swiveling in unison like the coordinated tentacles of a sea anemone. Any individual tentacle may take responsibility for pointing out a "bird," which is what they call indistinct flitting movements in the peripheral vision. After that the tentacles operate as a unit.

The group leader is responsible for conjuring up the birds, concentrating on "lifers," or birds that someone doesn't already have on his Life List of birds. "What do you need?" the leader will ask, and then track down the target birds somewhere in the vicinity. He or she does this through the use of alert ears and the same slack expression also noted in daydreaming students and the over-medicated. Once the target bird is located by ear, the leader draws him closer by means of an iPod playing the bird's song, which impels

the bird to get right up in his grill and point out that he's trespass-ing. This may seem like cheating. That's because it is cheating, but all the birders get a nice look, and the bird gets a "win" and a boost of confidence when the iPod shuts off.

This is known as "calling in" a bird, and, in fact, even at night, a group of birders can go out with an iPod set on "barred owl," and, if everyone remains very quiet, call in another group of birders with an iPod set on "barred owl." It's marginally satisfying.

Most birders, even the ones not qualified to lead a group, know a lot about birds. Many a time I found myself locked onto a bird, squeaking "birdbirdbird" in my usual coherent fashion, and someone would materialize behind me with a running narrative about the bird in question, like a proximity-animated audio tour in a museum. And some have specific areas of expertise. My friend Susan, for instance, is in the raptor-rehabilitation business. Susan wears eagles on her wrist. Susan's first inclination, upon spotting a mouse in her bathtub, is to go fetch one of her handy birds of prey to take care of the issue. If Susan, who has an enormous personality, only some of which is in her shirt, wants to impart some of her wisdom about birds, I intend to receive it and say *ma'am, yes ma'am*.

I was pleased once again to be in a beautiful Eastern deciduous forest, not as fernily voluptuous as an Oregon rain forest, but more diverse in many ways and more likely to host salamanders. There were drawbacks. The woods are not as dense as I'm used to, and a person has to hike a long way to be out of sight of the others. Who are, after all, scanning every inch of the territory with binoculars. So if you were to tip over while peeing (for instance), and gash your knee and soil your left shoe (say), there might not be anyone to help within earshot. (Theoretically.) However, it cannot be ruled out that you would be dead center in a spotting scope with a 30x magnification and under surveillance by a line of twenty fascinated people.

The bunching-up behavior of birders is best observed in a place like Cranberry Glade, a beautiful bog in which human traffic is confined to a narrow boardwalk. The birders bunch up at a warbler sighting, then break up and drift away only to bunch up later next to a waterthrush. Seen from above, and speeded up, they look like an embolism.

Another behavior that might be observed in a clot of birders is the tendency of one or more members to make a "pish-pish" sound in an effort to attract birds. (Collections of British gentlemen are distinguished by their ascots and beaks.) So, to recap, we have a group of people behaving in concert like a sea anemone wearing dorky paraphernalia and sounding like they have sprung a leak. We are not here to judge, people. Remember, birders are human, too, and they may well have a life list, but they do have a life. Also, a list.

I'm listless, but heaven help me, I've gone over. Now I'm going to be the person in the car in front of you slaloming over the highway with my head craned out the window looking straight up. Don't give me that look, Miss Cell Phone Blabbypants.

Die Hard, With A Backpack

It was August 3rd, the birthday of Andrea (the good niece). In her honor, Elizabeth (the bad niece) attempted to leave me for dead on the slopes of Mt. Rainier. She will probably say otherwise, but she can get her own dang blog.

To be absolutely fair, Elizabeth probably wasn't initially trying to kill me by hauling me up there. As she brought up on eight or nine dozen occasions that day, *I'm* the one who is famous for dragging people up mountains against their will. I don't mean to be difficult. It just so happens that a lot of the things I think are worth looking at are way up high, and we're down here practically at sea level, and I tend to believe anyone with sufficient peanut butter should be able to bridge the elevation gap. Furthermore, I like to believe that there are a lot of people out there who are secretly—very secretly—grateful to me for making them spend all day on a trail so steep you can reach out and touch it in front of you. At any rate, neither Elizabeth nor I suspected I'd be the one bounding up Mt. Rainier with all the gusto of a ninety-year-old asthmatic.

It didn't even start out well. We popped onto the trail with the usual vigor, and within a few hundred feet I made the announcement that I'd be slowing things down until I got my second wind. Turns out I didn't have one. I never kicked it into a gear past Trudge the whole day, and felt distinctly ill and fatigued to boot—the kind of feeling young people blame on what they'd imbibed the day before, and old people blame on being close to death. About halfway up, Elizabeth commented on our good weather. "Fwabbadabby bort," I observed. Elizabeth was alarmed. "Have you had enough water?" she wanted to know. "Biscorpal!" I assured her. "When was the last time you peed?" she asked—impertinently, I thought.

I flapped my hand limply downhill towards a point quite distant in both space and time. "You've got to drink more water, *now*," she insisted. "Bawa," I agreed. She uncorked the bottle and watched

me drain it, like a little Nurse Ratched dispensing meds in the loony bin. Elizabeth had never seen me this feeble and might have been a little worried. After all, she knew she probably couldn't dig more than a shallow grave in that rocky soil. We continued upslope at a glacial pace. I was enveloped by a vortex of flies who were probably trying to get a jump on things.

We finally crested a ridge at about four miles and were rewarded with meadows of flowers. "Look at those beautiful lupines!" Elizabeth enthused. "Boopings!" I agreed. Elizabeth brought out more water. I don't know where she found that goose-gavage tube she used to get it down my gullet. Still hadn't peed. We plodded onward, and were greeted heartily by a jaunty fellow at least fifteen years my senior. He was unbearably upbeat. "Hey, you're almost there!" he sang out. "Just a couple more little uphills and you'll hit the Wonderland Trail." He shrugged off a massive backpack and reclined against a tree, smiling. A couple more little uphills? Thanks, Pops. When you get back to civilization, have them send up a helicopter.

The two little uphills added another thousand feet of elevation gain, for a total of about 3700 feet in five miles. Pops was merely the first in a series of sturdy, smiling and thoroughly annoying septuagenarians, their legs churning like pistons. We met Pops one more time after we turned to go back. "Did you get to the lakes?" he wanted to know. We hadn't. "Good for you—leave something for the next time!" he said. *The next time.* I will say, he looked durned hard to murder.

I had put away about three quarts of water before I finally had to pee and Elizabeth left me alone. Looking back, I can only imagine that the previous week was to blame. I'd given a pint of blood, and it had been two hundred degrees in Portland for days on end, days in which I had drunk massive but apparently inadequate amounts of water. The human body is supposed to be more than seventy percent water, but I had done a little economizing and gotten it down to a nice tidy forty percent. All the cells in my body had gone gummy, and all the water I'd drunk on the trail had been devoted to re-inflating them, leaving the brain cells for last, before any had elected to tip into my bladder.

"You have to admit that those meadows on top were stunning," Elizabeth said. And I did have to admit that. They were almost as stunning as the ones we drove *right up* to the next day, *right* off the parking lot of the Paradise Lodge.

Merriweather

There were thousands of us bunched up in a gray little rest stop on the Washington side of the Columbia River. A fleet of busses had just shuttled us across the Astoria Bridge from Oregon, and we planned to walk right back, in an annual exercise called The Great Columbia Crossing.

It is worth noting that Lewis and Clark, after having withstood over seven thousand miles of hardship, were nearly done in after a few days in the rain here at the mouth of the Columbia. Their survival was in question; their clothes were a fright; they near perished from whininess. They had fetched up in a dot of a cove they called Dismal Nitch, and so it is called to this day, there being no compelling reason to change it. It was the very spot where we were now standing and jiggling for heat under a low slate sky. Dismal Nitch is south of Cape Disappointment and just around the bend from Go Stick Your Head In The Oven Bay. It's rainy.

This is the kind of trouble you might expect from an outfit calling itself the Corps of Discovery, bound and determined to discover things all on their own, when they could have asked anybody and they would have found out how rainy it is. The whole area is renowned for moistness, but they'd have done fine with a little raingear and a proper attitude. "This is the first of ninety consecutive days of rain," they might have said, "a good time to catch up on our reading."

Instead they came boating up wearing buffalo hides that promptly rotted away, and they got out of their canoes and into a giant snit.

It rained sideways for six days, which anyone could have told them is quite typical of November, and—as Clark described it—*our camp [was] entirely under water dureing the hight of the tide, every man as wet as water could make them all the last night and to day all day as the rain Continued all day…and blew with great violence immediately from the Ocian for about two hours.* Were this not Dismal enough, some of the party elected to drink salt water and *on them it acts as a pergitive.* Which probably put a capper on things.

At least they had salmon. Salmon spawn in tiny streams and make their way to the *Ocian*, where they live and grow for up to four years, and if everything goes just right, they return to the waters of their birth and become quite delectable in a lemon caper sauce, if they're not overcooked, and that's where most people go wrong. It's hard to beat a properly prepared salmon, and yet that is just what Lewis and Clark did; they subsisted on *dried fish pounded*, which pretty much defines overdone. Even if they had known what to do with a salmon, it's going to get on your nerves if you eat it every day, all winter long.

The native Chinook people, meanwhile, were high and dry, wearing clothing woven from the bark of cedar trees—essentially, they were wearing lightweight log cabins, and the rain just sheeted off them. They furnished the hapless Corps of Discovery with a steady supply of pounded salmon in an effort to turn the tide of invasion, but it was for naught. Soon enough there was an epidemic of white people everywhere you looked, and they began doing things Lewis and Clark couldn't even have dreamt of. Bottled water alone would have rendered them flabbergastric.

They also put in a magnificent bridge across the mouth of the Columbia, over which Lewis and Clark could simply have strolled to Oregon, not that it would have improved their mood any. They invented automobiles to stick on the bridge. And finally they came up with the Great Columbia Crossing. You can almost hear Lewis and Clark's minds blowing across the winds of history, but the fact is many odd activities become plausible when you do not have to slay your own dinner or repair your disintegrating buffalo attire on a daily basis.

On the day of the Crossing, half of the bridge was closed to automotive traffic. Modern people, especially in the blue states, love bicycle or pedestrian events that inconvenience motorists, and we swell with satisfaction when we see the line of cars creeping along sullen at our sides. For a short while, we have defeated the scourge of fossil-fuel dependence, and we swing our arms and thump our chests on our commemorative t-shirts.

It's a great feeling, well worth the two-hour drive from Portland.

The Numbers Racket

So this nice hippie lady was cooing over my garden from the sidewalk, and, as I always do, I invited her in. She was delighted. She liked every little thing and she particularly swooned over the raspberries, which were going like gangbusters. "Oh, would you like to pick some?" I asked. "I probably won't keep up. Let me get you a bucket." I got us each a bucket. We picked, we chatted.

Comes to pass that she considers herself very intuitive by nature, and has amplified her abilities by studying numerology. "What is numerology?" I asked, fairly certain, however, that it wasn't going to be anything I'd sign up for. My new friend was enthusiastic. Numerology was *only* the key to understanding one's role in the universe. She was all ready to demonstrate and asked me what my birthdate was, which I am always happy to divulge. (September 24, 1953, size eight, teal greens and turquoise.) She totted the numbers up.

"Oh! You're a three! Withdrawn, shy, distrustful, and a little on the stingy side," she said, decanting the bucket of raspberries into a paper sack and starting in on the re-fill. "That's unbelievable," I admitted.

"I *know!* It's truly amazing. I'm naturally a skeptical person, but the more I read about it, the more I realized how real this is. Pythagoras believed in it, and he, like, totally invented math!" He *was* very mathy, that's true. He is credited with discovering the right triangle, which is huge. Before Pythagoras, everybody's tables fell over.

Dave popped into the back yard to meet our new friend. I explained what we were talking about and suggested he toss his own birthday into the hopper. The raspberry lady performed her calculations. "Two. You're like an economics guy, right? Like a financial wizard, maybe a banker?" Dave is not allowed to pay the bills. It's only been recently we allowed him to have his own checking account.

"That's unbelievable," he admitted.

"I *know!*" she said. We'd picked most of the berries by then, and I told her to come on back in a couple days if she wanted more.

"Thanks for all the information," I told her. "The really amazing thing to me is that Pythagoras was able to get his own numbers right. How did he even know he was B.C.?"

"I *know!*" she said. "Spooky, isn't it?"

I had to look into this numerology business. It was even spookier than I thought. Pythagoras is reported to have been born between 580 and 572 B.C. I think this says more about his mother's abilities than it does his, but true to form, she gets barely a mention. Some oracle or other had predicted, when she was pregnant, that she would give birth to a wise and beautiful man. (Or at least an eight-year-old.) I took a look at a stone bust of him, and he did indeed have chiseled features.

So Pythagoras believed that everything in the universe worth knowing could be expressed mathematically, and that one's own numbers revealed much about oneself, including one's past lives. The best website I was able to find, based on the saturation of rainbow colors in the wallpaper, also made mention of Edgar Cayce, the "Sleeping Prophet of Virginia Beach." As the Napping Diva of NE 29th Avenue, I had to investigate further. Cayce was a psychic who reportedly had the "ability to put himself into some kind of self-induced sleep state by lying down on a couch, closing his eyes, and folding his hands over his stomach." This was stunning. I just so happen to have very similar abilities, except that I tend to list to the side and drool a little. Cayce was also reported to have been able to read the Akashic Records. I had to look that up. Turns out the Akashic Records are like a library of everything that has ever happened; like, as Wikipedia has it, a "universal filing system which records every occurring thought, word and action." It's the Internet! Which is *just what I was using*! Unbelievable. Well. I was sold.

I plugged some of my numbers into the on-line numerology form and read the results avidly. It cautioned me to avoid depression, jealousy and worry. You can't hang a price tag on that kind of advice. Then: "You aren't the type to retire because you need to keep expanding and enlarging." I felt really let down. I am not only retired, but totally the type, and if I'm still expanding and enlarging, I don't see how it's any business of the Numerology website.

I'm not going to give them my credit card numbers.

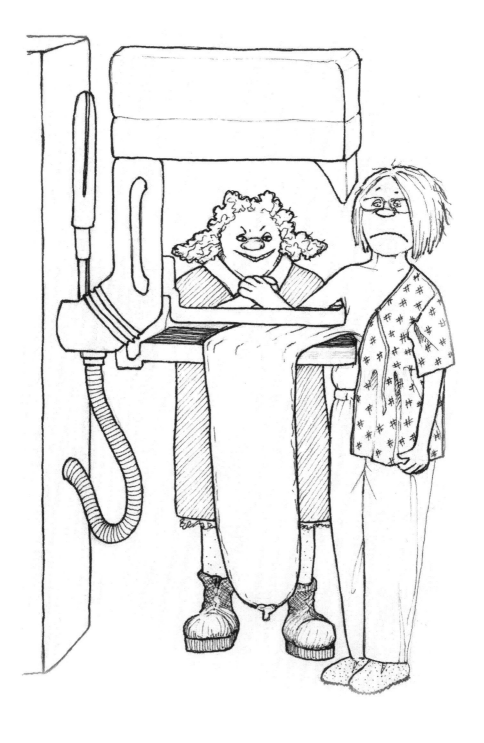

Pinned Down

I'm sitting on the cusp of Libra and Virgo, which puts me at risk of an astrological wedgie. But really I'm a Libra through and through. I hold the balances; I see both sides of an issue. I don't like to get pinned down. In spite of that, I just went in for my annual mammogram.

In the interest of my health, I have my annual mammogram every fifteen months or so. Fifteen-month years do wonders for your longevity. This time, after taking the required four pictures, they asked for a do-over. They said I moved. What moving? There's no moving. If the fire alarm goes off, I'm screwed. Nothing pins a girl down like a mammogram.

The woman in charge (let's call her Adolph) carefully stuffs your breast onto the bottom plate, hauling in a little extra from the belly, armpit and the lowermost of chins, and then takes the top plate and smashes you to a thickness that she can read through. The instructions are on the bottom plate.

This used to be more painful, but as one obtains maturity, as here defined by a marked decrease in sexual attractiveness, one's breasts begin to lose all their internal architecture, replacing it with a sort of apathetic goo. In the context of a mammogram, the procedure now involves less stuffing and cramming than merely peeling the tissue off the torso like a piecrust and rolling it out onto the plate. The top plate is now superfluous.

One year I got a letter afterwards suggesting I should come back in for a recheck. There was an "anomaly," and a date available in two weeks. I'm not the sort of person who can survive two weeks in a state of panic, so I badgered them until they admitted they weren't really doing anything just then, just sitting around eating pancakes and pita bread and playing with their food, and I raced in. The technician brought out my x-ray and hung it up on the wall for reference.

What these pictures used to look like, pre-menopause, with all the architecture intact, was something you might see from the Hubble telescope: millions of little stars and thready gases and nebulae, in which trained personnel can detect suspicious planets. I'd seen one of mine before. This one was deep space, all darkness, no nebulae at all, with the Star of Bethlehem blazing away right in the middle. I could see it from across the room. "Is that thing in the middle the anomaly we're looking at?" I whimpered, visualizing a tiny tumor glowing in a manger. The technician nodded. She used a more focused x-ray machine and zeroed in on my supernova. Then she left the room with the x-ray to show the doctor, leaving me with an inadequately distracting group of women's magazines. At times like these, one is no longer interested in how to keep pounds off during the holidays, or five new recipes for fried chocolate.

Adolph isn't allowed to tell you anything about your x-rays, even though you suspect she knows as much as the doctors do. She came back in and apologized that she needed to take a few more shots. Fifteen minutes later she came back and said she needed to escort me to stage two, Ultrasound.

By the time we'd reached the Ultrasound room, I had run through a number of items that needed changing in my will, and while she was consulting the doctor about the new results, I'd begun a preliminary list of music I thought would be nice for my funeral. She returned to accompany me and my breasts to stage three, a stern interrogation. The doctor had my old x-ray, the one with the big star, hung up next to a series of new ones, which were entirely blank. "As you can see," he said, using the pointer, "we can't find the anomaly anymore. We probably got a little pleat in there the first time. You don't seem to have anything in your breasts at all. You're good to go."

Nothing in them at all. I gave them an affectionate little pat, without taking my hands from my lap.

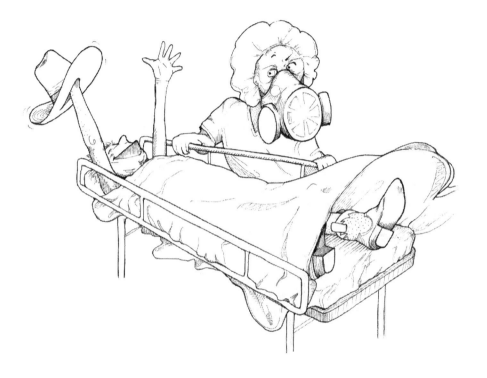

Music Of The Spheres

So I had my first colonoscopy right on schedule a few years back, and evidently I passed it with flying colors. Lord knows *something* passed with flying colors. And now they've started asking me to take more of a personal hand in my routine testing. This is why I was sent home from Kaiser with a small envelope containing everything I would need to collect my own stool sample and send it through the mail. I'm always getting shit in the mail, so it's sort of a novelty to send some back.

The thing is, this is one of those areas I've always preferred to leave to others. Maybe it's because I've never been a mom or a janitor, and I *have* been a baby—but if someone has to deal with what lands in the toilet, I'd rather it were someone else. The colonoscopy, for instance, didn't require all that much of me. My only role was the night before, and that wasn't really any big deal. You just do what comes naturally, only louder and with more pep. Once you've gotten to the clinic and have your gown on, your part is pretty much over with. In my case, I did come to, at some point towards the end of the procedure, and was able to watch some of the proceedings on a TV monitor and recognize what I was looking at. But I could tell I wasn't entirely back to normal because normal people do not blow "Oklahoma!" out their ass in a crowded hospital corridor. I recognized the opening note right away, and I discovered that if I exercised a little sphincter control—I believe trumpeters refer to that as "embouchure"—I was able to replicate the tune pretty well. I held onto the "O!" for as long as I could, and by the time the wind came sweepin' down the plain, I'd like to think I had everybody's attention.

The home stool sample kit comes with instructions that are pure literature:

Unfold and put the large collection tissue paper inside the toilet bowl on top of the water. (Don't use the small absorption pad included in the return envelope—you'll need that for something else later.)

Gripping! See how that keeps you on the edge of your seat? It's a page-turner.

Have a bowel movement so that the stool (feces) falls on top of the collection paper.

The paper takes up the entire interior of the toilet bowl. If you miss it, you were way too close to the edge of your seat.

Take a sample of your stool (feces) before it touches the water.

Fortunately, they don't mean in mid-flight. But frankly, seeing your stool plated up like an entrée and twirling a spoon in it sort of cancels out the entire beauty of having indoor plumbing. The instructions go on to say you can flush, and to ("please") wipe off the sample bottle if some sample has gotten on the outside. As a former mailman, I can endorse that request.

Dave got a kit at the same time I did, but he's just practicing for now. He's doubtful about the collection tissue paper and is pretty sure he could sink it in one shot. I think he can, too.

Round Feet

I don't know what it means to have flat feet. I'm probably missing something. It seems to me that flat is just exactly what your feet *should* be, especially on the bottom. If that keeps you out of the army, it's just a bonus.

I don't have problems with my feet, except first thing in the morning. Evidently they round up overnight. They're like little spheres, and walking on them flattens them out again, but that first morning trip to the bathroom is a bear. It's a rocking, rolling, reeling event, and I carom off the walls until they finally funnel me towards the toilet. After that, things flatten out nicely and I'm able to navigate just fine for the rest of the day.

I've spent a lot of time working on exercises designed to straighten out my foot strike and they've been largely successful. I can tell because I hardly ever keel over anymore when I'm putting on my socks. I never sit down to put them on for some reason, and it was always about a fifty-fifty proposition that I'd remain upright, especially when I was putting on the left one. I'd just tip right over. People said it was like watching a dinosaur die. Now that I've worked on my foot strike, I realize that I used to procrastinate or spelunk or whatever it's called when your ankle rolls in. Dave always asked me, as he was giving me a hand back up again, why I didn't just let go of my sock, and I really don't have a good answer for that, except that it simply never crossed my mind. My mission was to get my sock on, and I stayed focused on that mission all the way to the floor. Then I'd finish putting my sock on, get back up and get on with my day. It's just like figuring out how to do something on the computer. There may be a quicker, easier way, but you tend to stick with what works for you.

My friend Linder has many extraordinary qualities, but her feet are particularly dramatic. They are far from flat, but they're not round, either. The arches are so pronounced she could tuck a gerbil under each one and not hear a peep of complaint out of them all day. Also, her big toes are normal size, and instead of the rest of them tapering down like proper little piggies, they're all the same length, about half the length of the big ones. I'm sure it made bedtime rituals a lot easier on her parents when she was a baby. After the big one went to the market, it was nothing but "wee wee wee" all the way home. They're unusual enough that at one point, when she was completely undressed in the doctor's office, he suddenly yelled "Oh, my God, look at that! I've never seen anything *like* that before! Hey, Harry! Tom! Get in here, you've got to see *this!*" The fact that that doctor may still be alive to tell the tale, and in his original baritone, is evidence of many of Linder's extraordinary qualities.

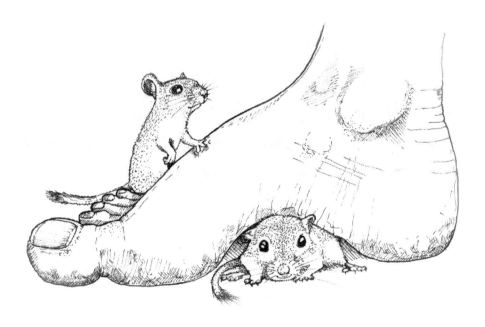

I miss Linder. I wish she lived here so she could have joined us for a sumptuous champagne brunch we had here recently. There was no particular occasion for it, except that we had several large bottles of cheap champagne left over from a party a few weeks ago, so six of us got together and put a nice dent in the stash. A real nice dent. Found out that champagne makes my feet round, too.

Chapter 7

Fun With Death

~

A Grave Matter
Abbie Normal
Bad Day At The Zoo
On Being A Foot Shorter
Hot In Portland
Loved Ones, With A Side Of Lefse
The Mortal Coil Shuffle
Murr: It's What's For Dinner
You Can't Keep A Good Man Down
Nearly Beloved

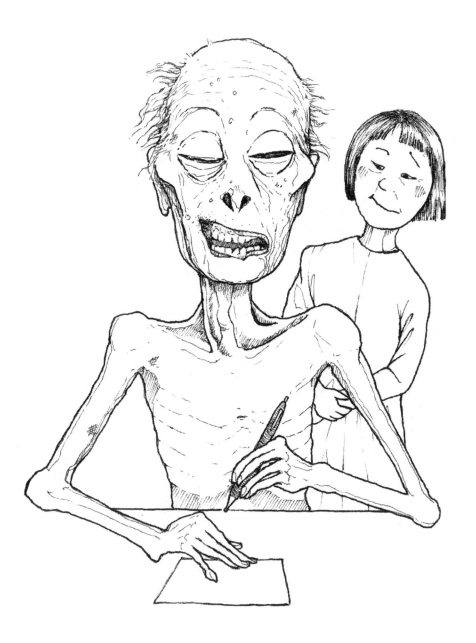

A Grave Matter

There's a scandal brewing over at Arlington Cemetery, with the Army reporting an unacceptable number of burial errors. Not the kind that involves burying soldiers who are not entirely dead, which tends to resolve itself in a few hours. This is a matter of mislabeled, unmarked or improperly marked graves. And this is a scandal because, as anyone who has even a rudimentary knowledge of zombies knows, we like to know where our dead people are at all times.

We go to great lengths to assure this, and always have, going back to the earliest days when some people marked the spot with an entire pyramid. Nowadays we mostly use stones and plaques and plastic petunias and teddy bears, but it's the same concept.

It's more important to some people than others. My siblings and I buried our parents somewhere in Bozeman, Montana, after first reducing them to an economical shoebox size, per their instructions. I visit each of them several times a day, but in thirty years I've never made the trip to the Bozeman cemetery, and I don't think they mind. The shoebox size takes up less space. We did the same thing with my sister, who would never have taken up much space anyway. Her ashes were turned into the soil of her bodacious vegetable garden, where she spent some of her best time, and now—I snuck a peek a year later—she is marked by a massive bean plant. I go back and forth on whether to tell the current homeowners why their vegetables are so big.

It did always strike me as an odd use of the scenery to plant people full-length in rows and rows, even though I enjoy walking in cemeteries. How is it we haven't run out of room? Apparently in many locations we have, and have taken to stacking up. They won't do it to people who are just a little dead, but the deader you are, I guess the less you mind.

Another way of taking up less space is to save only the head, which is standard procedure in cryogenically frozen people. I find the thought of preserving my head horrifying and would never consider it, unless maybe I'd had some work done. These people have arranged for this treatment beforehand in the hope that they can be revived when whatever killed them is cured, and they're okay with coming back as what can only be termed an extreme quadriplegic. One of these outfits dropped the ball a while back and accidentally thawed someone out, then refroze him, and his still-limbed relatives are hoppin' mad about it. But what if they come up with a cure for cancer and still haven't conquered freezer burn?

The problems at Arlington stemmed from the conversion of the records from paper to digital. They're lucky they only misrecorded some names. If I'd been in charge of the project they'd have to change the name of Arlington Cemetery to The Blue Screen Of Death. Still, I guess it's a horrible thing to go to all the trouble of visiting a loved one and trimming up the grass and putting out a jar of peonies only to find out that the target bones of your affection are several yards away. It's like voting for the Clear Skies Act and discovering it was really the Polluters' Preservation Initiative all along.

The whole matter becomes even more complicated if you're not sure if someone's even dead or not, which can happen if they watched a lot of TV. Not too long ago, the folks in Japan were out looking for their officially-oldest man and when they knocked at his door, they were turned away repeatedly by relatives who did not want to disturb his rest. It turns out he was already thirty years past disturbing, tucked into his bed with a blanket over his mummified remains. If people are old enough, they don't look much different than mummies, but still. You'd think his relatives would have noticed something when they tried to get him to sign the deposit slips for all those pension checks.

Abbie Normal

I don't know how many times I've said I wished I had my father's brains. I'm just glad I never mentioned that out loud at the funeral home.

A New Mexico family is suing (the hell out of) two funeral homes for giving them a little more service than they wanted. Their mother perished in an auto accident in Utah, and her remains and personal effects were bundled up by a local funeral home and sent to the New Mexico funeral home. On the day of the funeral, a box containing the dead woman's personal effects was solemnly passed to the family, who stowed it in their car, and there it stayed, unopened, until a day later when it acquired an aroma. There in the box was an assortment of personal items and a bag of brains. Mom's brains. We shall assume.

We shall not dwell overmuch on how the brains came to be separated from the rest of the body. It was by all accounts a dreadful car wreck. And someone has the unfortunate task of picking through the wreckage and gathering up items which should be returned to the surviving family members. Sunglasses, pearl necklace, rings, road map, little pine tree deodorizer, brains. *One of these things is not like the others. Do you know which one? Just off the top of your head?*

No one is saying her brains should have been ignored, and that can happen. If you will recall, Bob Crane, who played Col. Hogan in Hogan's Heroes, was murdered by bludgeoning in a case that remains unsolved. The detective on the case got so far as guessing that the murder weapon was a tripod, and he had a tripod-owning suspect who had rented a car on the night in question, but other than that he was stumped ("I know nothing," he probably said). Fourteen years later, someone discovered some brains in the rental car that had been overlooked the first time around.

"Whoa, Ned! Check it out!"

"I'll be go to hell. Looks like brains. Don't that beat all?"

"Well, put them back—we're looking for a signed confession, here. Focus! Focus!"

For its part, the funeral home in Utah defended its actions as standard procedure. According to misleadingly-named Serenicare's director, the redundantly-named Dick Johnson, "It is common practice to ship it inside a bag. If we put it back in [the head], it could have been a soggy, leaky mess." Whereas this is no doubt true, it may be the biggest example of Missing The Point since Sarah Palin's handler suggested she might be more comfortable in flats and a pantsuit. People! No one doubts you did a nice, tidy job of it. But this isn't Safeway, and that's not a pork roast. Don't put it in the cart.

Mr. Johnson went on to explain that in these situations the family is "typically encouraged to let the funeral home discard the bag rather than take it home with them," implying that there may have been a communications lapse on the New Mexico end. There seems to be some confusion all around, so I have taken the trouble of drafting some guidelines for funeral homes in the future:

Always keep in mind that we want to remember Mom as she was when alive. Most of us.

In circumstances like these, we would like other, unrelated people to get the spatulas and whatnot and get her scooped up, recombobulated and as presentable as possible and transported to a burial site.

This includes her brains.

Standard procedure is to bag up any brains that have strayed and insert them into the torso for shipping, just like gizzards in a Butterball.

We do not want to receive her brains along with her personal effects. Even if they are double-bagged.

Seriously. You can ask the next hundred people you meet, and not one of them is going to want a bag of their mom's brains. A rib-eye or a bit of brisket, max.

Bad Day At The Zoo

Everyone associated with the Rio Grande Zoo in New Mexico was horrified to discover their beloved giraffe Kashka had been dismembered and stuffed in a dumpster, but how else are you going to get a giraffe in a dumpster?

Kashka had recently been euthanized when she suffered a devastating leg injury after falling. It is not surprising that a simple fall might be more consequential to such a highly vertical animal, and Kashka was said to have had six calves, so that compounds the injury. There is a protocol involved, of course, with disposal of zoo animals. They are never tossed in the lion's cage: visitors do not appreciate that much Nature. And apparently there is no cemetery. This is certainly a relief to the grounds crew, inasmuch as a simple grave would not suffice for the likes of a giraffe, which would require a trench no matter how you fold it up. The standard procedure is to remove the dead animal to the local landfill. The zoo employee responsible for disposing of Kashka had, in fact, previously ushered a sea lion to the landfill, so he was no doubt familiar with the plan. But time gets tight, there's always an immense amount of clean-up to accomplish at any zoo, there's one's Facebook page to update, and let's face it: the contents of the dumpster do end up in the landfill. Nevertheless the employee was not commended for his efficiency.

It is hard to imagine how he was able to chop up the giraffe and get it in the dumpster without anyone knowing about it. But that is the story, and the zoo is sticking to it. The grisly discovery was made by the local garbage driver, who is said to have spotted the giraffe in the dumpster—at least the parts that weren't already spotted. He was taken aback.

It put me in mind of a similar caper in this area in the nineties. A woman was discovered to have murdered her boyfriend, cut him up into little pieces and, over time, flushed him down the toilet. According to her roommate, the woman had previously threatened to "blow him up," and spent a lot of time in her extremely foul-smelling bedroom, emerging occasionally with items in plastic bags. Furthermore, she carried a toilet plunger in her car, and there was a large "pool of organic matter" in the attic. All of this struck the authorities as suspicious. But what finally did her in was the discovery of boyfriend nuggets in the septic tank in the back yard. She might have gotten away clean if she'd just been on the sewer system.

I do feel for the garbage man at the zoo. It must have given him quite a start. Back when we had an adorable terrier dog, I clipped her fur every summer out in the back yard. On one of these occasions, I arranged her clippings into a terrier sculpture and left it out on the lawn. When Dave came home, he thought the dog had died. After we laughed about that, I woke up the next day and glanced out at the lawn and had the exact same reaction, and I was the one who put it there. We agreed to put the fur in the garbage can, where it horrified us both one more time each. That's four dead dog scares in two days. I'm sure it would have been even worse with a giraffe.

On Being A Foot Shorter

When I walked out with a shovel the other day and told Dave I was going to dig a big hole, he got a little nervous. "How big?" he wanted to know. "Six-five?"

Dave's counted on my reluctance to dig holes over the years, correctly suspecting that I'd tire long before I'd gotten his grave dug. But I just found out that it isn't really necessary to dig that big a hole. Maybe you've also read about James Hines, the fellow in South Carolina who, at 6'7", was too big for his casket, so the undertaker undertook to chop his feet off and wedge them in alongside his body. People are pretty upset about that undertaker, and

for good reason. What kind of person would do such a thing, when he could have cut the head off and placed it on his chest between his hands, where the lily usually goes? That would have had so much more dramatic impact when they exhumed the body.

The story does vindicate what Dave's been saying all these years, that they just don't make the world for tall people. That's why he has so many divots in his head, and doesn't like to fly. But there are many instances in which his height comes in handy. Not always; Dave has taken to stashing the toilet paper on top of the cabinet in the laundry room, a decision that's going to come back and bite him in the butt one of these days, when I run through a roll and can't replace it. But in general, when I need something off the top shelf, I stand under it pointing like a two-year-old, saying "Ehh, ehh, ehh," until he comes along to fetch things down for me. We call it using the "Extend-a-Dave." I wouldn't want anyone to think I think of him as just a tool, though, because I don't. No, the Extend-a-Dave is my *favorite* tool—that, and the little orange-peeler dealie.

Dave is a tall man, and I am neither, and for some reason it's a lot more entertaining to poke fun at the little person than it is to do the opposite. So I've been the recipient of quite a lot of friendly abuse for quite a while now. Mostly I take it in stride, however short a stride. Once or twice, out of sheer crankiness, I haven't been in the mood. I told him during one of those episodes that I would appreciate it if he could lay off the short jokes for just a little while. He apologized with what seemed like genuine remorse, and then quietly said, after a few moments, "I thought most of those jokes were over your head anyway."

If you'll excuse me, I have a bit more digging to do.

Hot In Portland

The second sound you heard the other evening was the sound of me weakly stabbing myself in the head with an ice pick. The first sound was my neighbor saying "it's supposed to get down to 104 degrees tomorrow."

In other news:

It is not possible to lay your wrist veins open with an oscillating fan. The blades just quit.

The cord from the ceiling fan is not strong enough to hang from.

Spoiled fruit will not kill you outright.

If you put your head down and charge straight into the pointy corners of the refrigerator, it feels pretty good until you come to again.

Thighs can be removed from a plastic lawn chair by gently inserting an ice pick under the edges and prying up. To remove skin from a metal lawn chair, allow to bake until crisp (fifteen minutes), scrape up with a spatula, add barbecue sauce and serve.

All the doorknobs are hot. Just open it and go in.

Just because the toilet seat is unusually warm, it doesn't mean it's turning Japanese. You can wait all day, and it's not about to squirt water at you or dry you off. You're still on your own.

Your local newspaper is offering helpful tips to cope with the heat, right on the front page. "Wear Sun Hat" is one, accompanied by a helpful drawing of a sun hat. "Seek Shade" is another. There is a helpful drawing of a generic tree in profile with a dark spot next to it, an arrow pointing at the dark spot. You are one of the last fifteen people who still subscribe to your local newspaper, and your local newspaper suspects you are a moron.

Black cat fur absorbs heat. Fur can be removed from the thighs with a damp sponge. Cats can travel about fifteen feet in the air before returning to earth. The bandaids are in the pantry.

There is a temperature above which your computer tower will actually begin to pant. Windows Vista, however, still freezes.

About ten degrees before the point at which life ceases to exist, humor dies. I am not funny. You are definitely not funny.

Why, yes, it IS hot enough for me, thank you! Ha ha! Have you met Mr. Ice Pick?

Loved Ones, With A Side Of Lefse

There is a perennial ad in the obituary section of the newspaper for "funeral alternatives." I'm always drawn to that, since I consider every day to be a funeral alternative of a sort, and I'd like to keep that up. Turns out there are a number of different ways to dispose of a corpse, beyond the traditional methods of embalming and burial, cremation, and concrete boots.

You have that option of being shot out into space, which is nice if you want your legacy to be "I could have rid the world of malaria, but I thought it would be more fun to be shot out into space." Or, in another option available to those with wealth afflictions, you could be frozen cryogenically and thawed out when a cure for your terminal illness is discovered. I always imagine that departed soul floating around quite peacefully, maybe shivering a bit, but happy enough, and then being yanked back into a world of chemo and woe.

There are other possibilities. I am informed that the state of Oregon is considering regulation of a number of new "death care consultants." Among the alternatives out there is the practice of freeze-drying a corpse and turning it into a fine powder, drying it, and putting it into a potato muffin. That would be just the ticket if you want to take your loved one camping. Oh wait, that's potato *coffin*. Still.

And there are a number of companies in the business of dissolving bodies into a sort of soapy goo. They're calling this "resomation," but you can't fool me—I'm half Norwegian. That's lutefisk.

If I absolutely did have to choose for myself, I guess I'd want to be tossed into a peat bog. A body buried in a peat bog barely deteriorates at all. Thousand-year-old corpses have been unbogged and found to look like they're just a little tired, maybe just a little squashed up. That's how I look first thing in the morning already.

But for the record, if I go before you all do, please note that I do not care what you do with me. As long as I'm still topside I would like to be fed and watered regularly but after that it's going to be entirely up to you. I do think it's a nice touch to be an organ donor. Even skin is harvestable, and there are parts of me that could cover a lot of territory. My eyes probably wouldn't be worth much, except as a novelty to the far-sighted. I've got two perfectly serviceable kidneys. My liver is heroic. Three people could get new chins.

The Mortal Coil Shuffle

According to researchers at the Dana-Farber Cancer Institute in Boston, patients who relied on religious faith were three times as likely as others to ask for and receive life-prolonging care, such as mechanical ventilation or CPR, in the final week of life. A friend of mine was surprised. He thought these people should have had the most to look forward to. I suppose they wouldn't have come up with something to look forward to if they weren't so terrified of being extinguished.

It's natural enough. Most of us, in the face of all evidence to the contrary, believe we are very important, and as such deserve to go on pretty much forever. So throughout history, a lot of effort and imagination have gone into this enterprise of opting out of death. People ride comets, wear special underwear, get buried with treasure. Bribes, essentially—in case Heaven is something like Chicago.

Eternity doesn't always last as long as you'd think. The River Styx is undoubtedly a dry creekbed by now. The famous deal with the 72 virgins is fine as far as it goes, but it would only be good for about a month or so—you know, depending. There's one religion you might consider signing up for where you get your own planet. That's the one where you live with your family for ever and ever, so you're going to want to read the fine print. When it comes to Eternity, there are as many destinations as there are ways to go. In most cases, they're Members-Only clubs.

Most people just go with whatever mythology they grew up right next door to, and tend to look down their snoots at the others. My

neighborhood religion fancied a harp for every soul. That's about as close to hell as this piano player cares to imagine, so I may have strayed from the orthodoxy early on.

I'm not any more interested in dying than anyone else is, but it makes more sense than the alternative, if you think about it. There is something appropriate about death. It makes life just a little more attractive when it has an artful frame around it. Otherwise eternity seems a little crowded and unkempt, and the script of life might as well be written on toilet paper stuck to a shoe. Forever.

So I have spent very little of my adult life beagling around for an out. The way I see it, if I can't even get my socks to match up out of the dryer, I don't know why I should presume to have any insight into the hereafter. And I thoroughly expect to slide out of this gig without a bus in sight or a ticket to ride. But I think about this splendid universe most every day, smiling hard, and think: "Huh. Don't that beat all."

That other stuff is for people who can't take "huh" for an answer.

Murr: It's What's For Dinner

I am proud of knowing someone from Newfoundland, a region whose existence has only been verified in my lifetime. My friend Sara is a repository of disturbing facts, among which is the revelation that people in her part of the planet eat Murrs. Or not murrs, precisely, but murres, the dashing and athletic sea bird with the dapper black-and-white outfit, shapely rear end and world-class sense of humor. Only they do not call them murres, but "turrs." It would seem odd to mispronounce a word like "murre" in this way unless you take into account that in Newfoundland, above-freezing is not their native temperature, and initial consonants can be unpredictable.

Besides, my own name only came about because the people I went to college with couldn't pronounce "Mary," so we've got no room to complain. Its spelling is thus arbitrary, and has been reinterpreted variously as Myrrh, Muir, Murre, Merv, Merle, and Sally. Nevertheless, it's mine now, and I'm not sure how I feel about being fried up with carrots and potatoes.

I do know that I'm not likely to partake of one myself. That's not out of any allegiance to murres, but because Sara says they're greasy and stringy. There is a bit of a taboo about eating your own kind, though, most places. It's frowned upon in America, for instance, which is a quite typical attitude in countries marked by obesity. The subject probably never comes up in your more gristly populations. But survey a random sampling of Americans and you're likely to find they think human meat tastes immoral.

Actually, the flavor is probably not the problem. Human meat is called "long pig" and is reputed to be delightful. There are contradictory texts, however. In the Bible, it is reported that during the famine in Samaria, two women agreed to boil and eat their sons, and the first woman did so, and shared the meat. But the next day the other woman refused to fry up her own son. So maybe it was not so palatable after all.

No one really knows how prevalent the long-pig cuisine is, worldwide. There is evidence of it in Neanderthal populations, where a good eyebrow roast could go a long way. In my youth, cannibalism was depicted fairly often. The typical scene in 1955 A.D. (30 B.P.C.) shows a duo of white men, one of whom is usually Bob Hope, in a large stewpot attended by dark chefs whose accoutrements are made of disassembled skeletons. Nowadays it is rare to medium-rare to see such a portrayal.

Some cannibalism was observed during the days of Christopher Columbus, and when Queen Isabella decreed that Spanish colonists were only allowed to enslave natives who were cannibals, their numbers spiked dramatically.

I'm probably not as averse to the practice as most people; at least I'm not willing to reject it out of hand. "How can you even think about eating a human being?" I've been asked, and I'm not entirely sure how to answer that, but I do know butter and salt would have to be involved. For all I know, I've already had some. When someone does all the cooking for you, you don't ask a lot of questions. The main reason I'm against it in general is out of self-preservation. I'd be the first to go. Some of my flesh is already falling off the bones. When people seem to be giving me their full attention as I rattle on about this or that, they might well be thinking: "mmm. Juicy. Good cracklin's."

You Can't Keep A Good Man Down

In March, 2010, Tassos Papadopoulos, the former president of Cyprus, was lowered into his grave after succumbing to lung cancer. The actual succumbing occurred fourteen months earlier, followed shortly by his first burial. A year almost to the day after he was originally laid to rest, he turned up missing. The marble slab covering his grave had been moved and the ground disturbed. Authorities were perplexed. Ordinarily, people lose a lot of their value upon their death, just like a new car leaving the sales lot, and it only keeps going down as time goes on. Even Mr. Papadopoulos' adherents could not be expected to miss him so gravely as to dig him up.

This has not always been the case. In prior centuries, body-snatching was quite the thing. Medical schools and scientists had a need for cadavers for dissection purposes, and the so-called Resurrection Men did a good business exhuming bodies to sell. Although this was illegal, it was not considered that heinous a crime to steal bodies once their previous occupants were done with them. Even then, though, the bodies lost value quickly, and efforts were made to retrieve only the freshest, leading some of the more ambitious entrepreneurs to introduce efficiencies by dabbling in murder, which was frowned on, especially when the victims were nice and white.

So in Cyprus, when the year-old corpse was dug up, no one knew what to make of it. Other than the marble slab, there had been no particular effort to protect the grave. It's a far cry from the ancient Egyptian standard, whereby the bodies of kings were elaborately sheltered from harm, both from the living and in the afterlife. Pyra-

mids covered labyrinthine tombs; the bodies themselves were embalmed and carefully enveloped in linen. Early on, Greek culture demanded similar customs for the more exalted personages, who were entombed after being lovingly wrapped in grape leaves, but the practice was largely abandoned in modern times when people found the yogurt dip off-putting. Mr. Papadopoulos was clearly left vulnerable.

But what was the nature of this crime? It was just another puzzlement, much like the local burglary ring that targeted nunneries, or the Post-It graffiti gang. Perhaps the body was being held for ransom, but it is unclear whether the family had been approached. A local government office was rumored to have received a small package with a severed, decomposed ear and a note made up of letters cut from magazines, but the message was Greek to them and no one in the mail room could figure out why someone would send them an old mushroom, so it had been discarded.

Acting on a tip, authorities recently found the body in a new, freshly dug grave on the edge of town, and after positive identification, it was reburied in the original grave, attended by family and supporters who shouted "Immortal! Immortal!" during the ceremony. This struck many as being an odd observation to make about a person who is being buried for the third time, but people have different perspectives on this sort of thing.

Three men were ultimately fingered for the dastardly deed, including one who allegedly directed the operation from jail. He was serving time for the rape and murder of two women, and had previously escaped for over a month before being recaptured. After the new accusation was leveled, he is reported to have threatened a hunger strike, but thought better of it after jail officials seemed insufficiently upset about it. He is now mulling his options, which include Sitting Stone-faced With Arms Folded During Skit Night, and Cutting Down On Sweets.

Nearly Beloved

Even when I was little, I read the obituaries. The Washington Post used to print some that started out with a one-word sentence: "Suddenly." Those were the ones I was looking for. They pushed every mortal button I had. A child does not even want to think about "suddenly." But I couldn't look away. I never saw one that started out "Gradually," although that probably applied at least as often.

When I first began reading the obituary column in the Oregonian, most of the information was contributed by family and edited for clarity. Among the things I noticed right away is that, apparently, people in North Dakota come here to die. Nearly one in ten people who show up in our obituary column were born in North Dakota. Inasmuch as there are only three or four hundred people living in North Dakota, this is a striking statistic. In North Dakota, where the phrase "he bought the farm" means he bought an actual farm, the phrase "he moved to Oregon" must have a sinister connotation. "Shame about Ole," they'd say at the coffee shop, "he was doing poorly all winter, and then he finally moved to Oregon."

The format of our local paper's obituaries has changed from time to time over the years, and recently, in a very wise marketing move, they have been stripped down to the very basics: name, birth, death, occupation, survivors, and details of disposition. It wouldn't matter if you'd lived to be a hundred or died in your first week; your obituary is the same length. There's your slid-out date, your keeled-over date, and the points in between put as tersely as possible. *Alexander Graham Bell. March 3, 1847-August 22, 1922. Al was in communications.* There you have it.

If you're a recently deceased person, there are only two ways to get any ink in the Oregonian. One is to be aligned with one of your fussier religions. A recent example starts out normal and then hits its stride in the third line: "Colleen is survived by her daughters Eileen, Patricia, Mary Claire, Mary Celeste, Mary Elizabeth, Mary Margaret, Mary Mary, Shirley, Goodness and Mercy, and her sons, Francis X., Patrick, Dominic, Ryan and Thomas." Picking up speed by line four, we are informed that "Visitation will be from 10am to 5pm Friday, Oct. 30th, in Boswell's Funeral Parlor, and again from noon to six on the following Saturday, followed by the recitation of the rosary, a funeral mass in the chapel, bingo in the basement, a reception in the Valley View Memorial Park and committal in the adjoining mausoleum." This is an obituary with legs. The entire thing shoved some poor Methodist all the way down to the bottom of the page up against a cremation ad.

The other way, and here's where the marketing comes in, is to have your survivors write a proper obituary and pay for it at the rate of 75 bucks an inch. I've taken the liberty of jotting down a few thoughts for my own obituary out of consideration for my survivors, and also out of dread that someone will memorialize me using a misplaced apostrophe.

Suddenly. Murr Brewster succumbed on the eve of her 100th submission attempt to "New Yorker" magazine after a long and cowardly battle with hypochondria.

Right up until the day of the unfortunate paper-shredder incident, Murr was notable for frequent declarations of groundless optimism. Her sunny affirmations in the face of adversity inspired many a person to want to rip her lips off, and indeed, nothing really rotten ever seemed to happen to her. She is universally credited by her many annoyed friends and acquaintances with skewing the curve of fortune, to the detriment of everyone else.

Per Ms. Brewster's request, her julienned remains will be dipped in cheese, boxed up and sent to all the major publishing houses in New York City. The bonier bits will be added to the soil in the tomato patch in a last-ditch attempt to thwart blossom-end rot, and the entire bed mulched with the manuscripts of her four unpublished books. This will either produce a perfect tomato or it won't, and either way, she doesn't need to hear about it.

Murr is survived by nearly six cases of beer after a recent trip to Costco, so in addition to the spontaneous celebrations that have already sprung up all over town, the official event will be at her house. We expect to have the door pried open by three; reminiscences and toasts should be wrapping up by 3:10, and looting can begin any time after that.

Murr Brewster is a retired letter carrier with a vestigial biology degree. She lives with her husband Dave and (technically) stuffed dog Pootie in Portland, Oregon. She bought her first Mobile Cellular Telephone in April, 2012 and is looking forward to learning how to retrieve her voice mail. When she is not picking at her hair and staring at birds outside her window, she is writing novels and short humor essays.

For more stuff and blather, please visit Murrmurrs at
murrbrewster.blogspot.com

Vivi **Reidler** Gerritsen is a graphic designer, advertiser, painter, publisher, and educator. She is the creative boss and owner of Blugredo, a graphic design and publishing company dedicated to those who would rather write a book than be overwhelmed by the details of self-publishing. Blugredo prepares your finished texts for publishing, develops book covers, and offers other essential design services. Learn more at [**www.blugredo.com**].

Vivi is currently living in Pittsburgh, Pennsylvania with husband Dave and a Playstation® machine. She is not really Russian.

Made in the USA
Charleston, SC
20 December 2012